From the Komaro, a series of paintings from the Peloponnese coast, by Jean-Philippe Delhomme, 2016.

'I also have Visa socks from a gas station in the middle of Thailand, a life-size Chinese medical doll,
fake crossover products from counterfeit markets in China or Brazil, like Chanel Converses, and of course dozens of different
Louis Vuitton–inspired bags, the further from the real the better.'
Cyril Duval, Tokyo. Interview by Simon Castets. Photography by Hanayo. 2009.

Opposite: Portrait of a house, Berry. Painting by Jean-Philippe Delhomme. 2015.

'A lot of the kids passing through were transient, and it was good that New York had somewhere they could stay.
The space was there for them. It felt like it was already theirs.'
The Spectrum club in Bushwick, New York City. Interview by Michael Bullock. Photography by Daniel Terna. 2016.

'I was in control before, so the apartment was a lot more twisted, and there was stuff everywhere.
Really, I mean, really a lot of stuff. Rather jammed. Then Victoire took over, and she threw everything away.'
Victoire de Castellane & Thomas Lenthal, Paris. Interview by Haydée Touitou. Photography by Frederike Helwig. 2016.

'I guess I enjoy hanging out there because we made an effort to make this place comfortable and inviting. We moved into this flat when I was pregnant—we were preparing ourselves for a new lifestyle, even though we had no idea how it would be.'
Madoka & Ola Rindal, Paris. Interview by Julie Cirelli. Photography by Ola Rindal. 2011.

'It's hard to remember when I first started helping my dad. Now, in my memory, it seems like there was never a time that the patio or the carport wasn't converted into a workshop ... The house was finished in 1950. Perhaps I was two or three years old. I'm sure I would have been around during the construction, but I have no memory of it.'
Peter Shire, Los Angeles. Interview by Matt Paweski & Ryan Conder. Photography by Ye Rin Mok. 2014.

Valentine Fillol-Cordier, London. Text by Jonathan Heaf. Photography by Kasia Bobula. 2011.

'Ideal weekend: four days long. Enough time for boredom to happen. No plans. Nap on the couch during the day … Not shopping. No TV.
No emotional need for the internet. Reversing the power relations between myself and my dog.'
Mike Mills, Los Angeles. Text by Mike Mills. Photography by Ye Rin Mok, 2008.

Felix Friedmann, London. Interview by Marco Velardi. Photography by Felix Friedmann. 2008.

Opposite: 'I love this excuse, "I collect, therefore I can burn shitloads of cash because I'm building a collection".
It comforts me. I'm like an old lady and a kid at the same time.'
Lovefoxxx, São Paulo. Text by Lovefoxxx. Photography by Luiza Sá. 2010.

'Because of this courtyard, the idea of nature comes into the book I'm writing a lot more. I even put the cottage in the book; it's owned by an old man who looks nothing like me, hopefully, and he actually gets killed in the cottage. I hope I have not written my own fate.'
Christopher Bollen, New York City. Interview by Michael Bullock. Photography by Kiko Buxo. 2008.

'My aspiration is to create poetry with anything I put my hands on, be it sculpture, architecture, or space.
What interests me is that the final result can become a poem, which is for me the mother of everything.'
Xavier Corberó, Barcelona. Interview by Albert Moya. Photography by Daniel Riera. 2015.

Audrey Fondecave-Tsujimura, Tokyo. Text by Audrey Fondecave-Tsujimura. Photography by Taro Hirano. 2009.

'Perhaps the primal reason that moved me to start building was that I found the last fine spot on a street in Esplugues …
I thought that if I could conceal the ugly bit, it could end up looking pretty nice. And that's how I have spent the past 50 years of my life.'
Xavier Corberó, Barcelona. Interview by Albert Moya. Photography by Daniel Riera. 2015.

'I still feel hippie, but I'm not a hippie on the outside. It just wasn't enough. It didn't work.'
Armin Heinemann, Ibiza. Interview and photography by Nacho Alegre. 2015.

Opposite: 'We started to walk up the marble cantilevered steps, the rail being nothing but the trunk of a young tree
that became thinner to the grip as you reached the upper levels.'
Feature on Neoptolemos Michaelides, Nicosia. Text by Michael Anastassiades. Photography by Hélène Binet. 2014.

'I work more at my desk than anything else in my apartment, so there's not much cocooning.'
Elein Fleiss, Paris. Interview by Marco Velardi. Photography by Aya Yamamoto. 2008.

Opposite: 'I was making fun of the idea of spirituality and abstraction, critiquing the work and heritage of the movement,
which was that abstract painting was a gateway to sublime transcendence.'
Peter Halley, New York City. Interview by Jim Walrod. Photography by Jeremy Liebman. 2014.

'Every object other than art should be utilitarian. The house is funny in that it's not really an object, it's more like a function.'
Klaus Biesenbach, the Rockaways, New York. Interview by Michael Bullock. Photography by Benjamin Fredrickson. 2016.

'I like white because it makes everything else on it look precious; black in the basement because it makes people look more sexy.'
Terence Koh, New York City. Text by Alex Gartenfeld. Photography by Nacho Alegre. 2008.

'You buy something and then you have to decide what you value. Do you want to keep the authority of the art object, which also in some ways renders the object impotent, or do you actually want to have a relationship with it—even at the risk of undermining its value?'
Andrea Zittel, Joshua Tree. Interview by Alix Browne. Photography by Ryan Lowry. 2016.

Opposite: 'In my case, all you see fits into a van, and it takes 25 minutes to put it in.'
Yorgo Tloupas, London. Interview and photography by Marco Velardi. 2008.

'This lobby is green because that's the first colour I looked at when we needed to paint it. You can actually see it from the street, nine floors down.'
Michael Stipe, New York City. Text by Michael Stipe. Photography by David Belisle. 2013.

Opposite: 'You're not going to find the answers by thinking about art all the time.'
Liam Gillick, New York City. Interview by Leon Ransmeier. Photography by Jeremy Liebman. 2016.

'Our building has 14 floors, is greyish-white, and has hundreds of square windows, which looks bizarre from the streets of Shibuya. Public housing *otakus* (i.e., nerds) call these sorts of buildings "waffles".'
Tenko Nakajima, Tokyo. Text by Tenko Nakajima. Photography by Tony Cederteg. 2013.

'Manuel and I are actually thinking of swapping rooms with our two daughters.
We only use our big room for our clothes and sleeping. They could do so much more with it.'
Shirana Shahbazi, Zurich. Interview by Daniel Morgenthaler. Photography by Lukas Wassmann. 2015.

'It isn't uncommon to find a giant mirror ball beside a huge green fist, both rescued from a friend's failed sustainable disco campsite venture.'
David Piper, London. Text by David Piper. Photography by Marco Velardi. 2009.

'My mother was an interior designer. She taught me how to position objects to create a sense of balance.'
Marcelo Krasilcic, New York City. Interview by Michael Bullock. Photography by Marcelo Krasilcic. 2011.

'Some people prefer brand newness. I like brand newness, too. But it would be like war to incorporate modernity into this environment.'
Kembra Pfahler, New York City. Interview by Michael Bullock. Photography by Vincent Dilio. 2016.

'Proust had really bad taste in that sense. He used his aunt's furniture—I mean, he didn't care at all.'
Alessandro Mendini, Milan. Interview by Gianluigi Ricuperati. Photography by Piotr Niepsuj. 2017.

'In a world as atomised as our contemporary one, it is nothing but encouraging to hear of a man who works tirelessly to prove to us that a stranger is just a friend you haven't met, fallen in love, married, and had babies with as a result of his dinners.'
Jim Haynes, Paris. Text by Anja Aronowsky Cronberg. Photography by Nacho Alegre. 2011.

'When he arrived home after a long night out and realised he still had some change in his pocket, he tragically announced,
"It's my end! I always used to outlast the money".'
Paulo César Pereio, São Paulo. Text by Alexandre Fehr. Photography by Richard Jensen. 2009.

Linus Bill, Bienne. Text and photography by Linus Bill. 2008.

'We never open the blinds. We just opened them for your visit. We put a protective UV film on the windows,
and the curtains are from El Puma's time. And we never turn off the air conditioning.'
Ruth & Marvin Sackner, Miami. Interview by Leah Singer. Photography by Ryan Lowry. 2015.

'Living here with 20 doormen and whatever is kind of extravagant to me.'
Raymond Pettibon, New York City. Interview by Leah Singer. Photography by Terry Richardson. 2014

'When I first came to New York, what was important to me was interviewing Richard Prince or having Barbara Kruger come to my studio—
that was success. I felt that exhibiting and having a voice in the world would come from those experiences, and it did.'
Peter Halley, New York City. Interview by Jim Walrod. Photography by Jeremy Liebman. 2014.

Opposite: 'Whether it be a neighbourhood, furniture, or even something that tastes good—at this point I'm just looking
for anything that I can protect to call my own.'
Jim Walrod, New York City. Interview by Patrick Parrish. Photography by Jeremy Liebman. 2012.

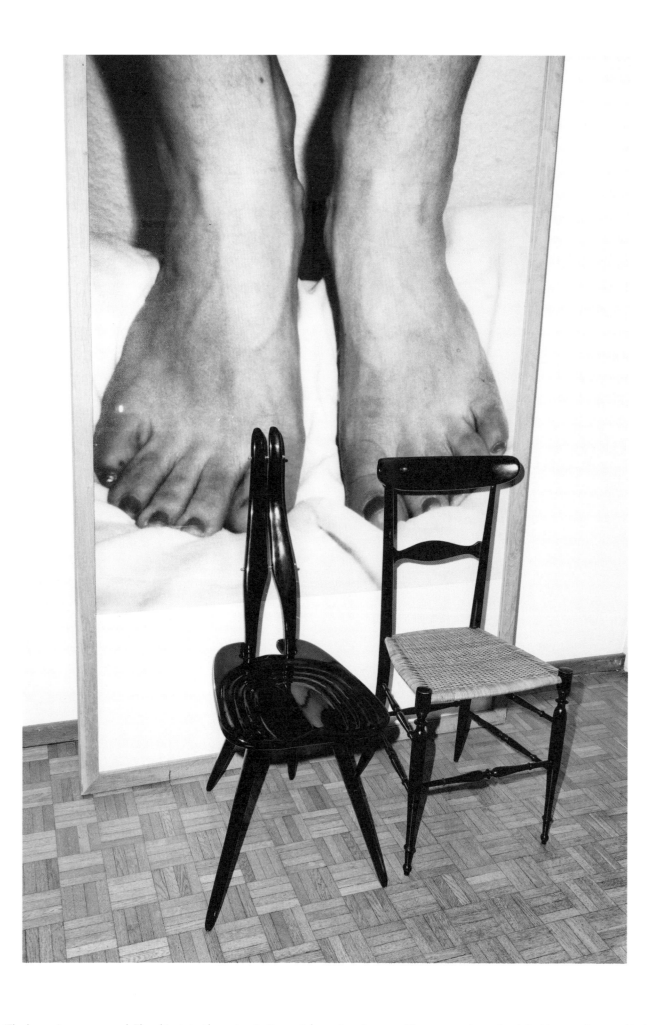

'The house is very personal. The objects inside are inspiration, not decoration. In a way, it's a personal scrapbook that I can walk around in.'
Beda Achermann, Zurich. Interview by David Torcasso. Photography by Walter Pfeiffer. 2011.

'I'm totally predatory when it comes to flea markets and junk shops ... I often dream about an object and then find it on my next rummage.
I have a lot of psychic energy that I put to good use.'
Zoe Bedeaux, London. Interview by Anja Aronowsky Cronberg. Photography by Juergen Teller. 2011.

'The second floor hosts one studio for Terence and one for Garrick, white with a mirrored coffin and a swastika spray-painted in gold on the shades, furnishing delicate accents.'
Text by Alex Gartenfeld, New York City. Interview by Alex Gartenfeld. Photography by Nacho Alegre. 2008.

'When parents go away to their *datcha* or somewhere else for a week or so, guys always invite a lot of guests.
You can spend about two or three days partying there, and then the same again to clean up the flat afterwards.'
Gosha Rubchinskiy, Moscow. Interview by Alexander Elzesser. Photography by Gosha Rubchinskiy & Pavel Milyakov. 2010.

Sara Sachs & Frederik Jacobi, Copenhagen. Text by Maria Gerhardt. Photography by Ada Bligaard Søby. 2013.

Opposite: 'I got a bit of a fright at first but I love it now.'
Marguerite Stephens, Johannesburg. Interview by Matthew Freemantle. Photography by Nico Krijno. 2015.

'I need a room for my canaries and for, like, the cats to loll around in.'
Martha Stewart, Bedford. Interview by Laura Regensdorf. Photography by Terry Richardson. 2016.

Opposite: Beda Achermann, Zurich. Interview by David Torcasso. Photography by Walter Pfeiffer. 2011.

'I walked in and immediately felt like I was home. It had low ceilings and many details that were reminiscent of homes
I'd grown up in and around in Connecticut. It felt like a womb.'
Chloë Sevigny, New York City. Text by Chloë Sevigny. Photography by Lele Saveri. 2009.

Opposite: 'It was a present from a friend of my girlfriend. She's Russian, she came to New York and stayed with us for a bit,
and as a thank you, she said, "I have the perfect present for you".'
Alex Wiederin, New York City. Interview by Katherine Clary. Photography by Nacho Alegre. 2010.

'In Hove, I choose to have books strewn and displayed in this way rather than on bookshelves so that one might see the relationship between them and read their carefully chosen "sea-themed" titles. The adage "never choose a book by its cover" is turned on its head here.'
Maureen Paley, Hove. Interview by Vince Aletti. Photography by Ana Cuba. 2017.

'The shapes are all taken from actual things, like lamps, boiled sweets, and, yes, even razor blades.'
Esther Mahlangu, Weltevreden. Interview by Matthew Freemantle. Photography by Nico Krijno. 2012.

Opposite: 'I used to travel with my own sheets, my own bed, just to recreate something a bit familiar everywhere I was going.'
François Halard, Arles. Interview by Nacho Alegre. Photography by François Halard. 2013.

'When the deal was done, Bob cried, "How can we support all this?" I was frantic; we had a 15-month-old son and a monster of a house,
and I had a husband saying, "I don't know what we're doing here".'
Denise Scott Brown, Philadelphia. Interview by Amelia Stein. Photography by Maya Handley. 2015.

Opposite: 'Underneath reality there is only chaos. That has to do with Wittgenstein threatening Popper with a poker in Cambridge.'
Fernando Arrabal, Paris. Interview by Pau Guinart. Photography by Josep Fonti. 2016.

Jack Pierson, New York City. Interview by Amelia Stein. Photography by Victoria Hely-Hutchinson. 2014.

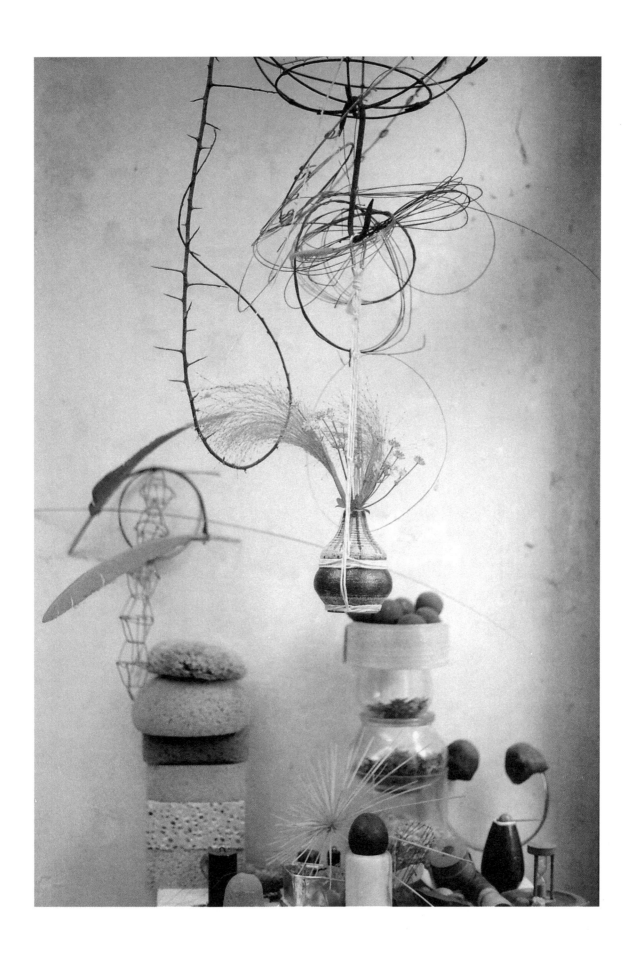

'It's a mess—but a beautiful and telling one. We are surrounded by unaccountable compositions of small objects, mostly stones.'
Guy Rombouts, Antwerp. Text by Koen Sels. Photography by Mieke Verbijlen. 2015.

Opposite: 'Where I used to see a perfect corner, now I see clutter. I'm slowly, unconsciously convincing myself that I'll eventually have to leave this place.'
José León Cerrillo, Mexico City. Interview by Michael Bullock. Photography by Nacho Alegre. 2012.

'Just before we came to the Milan fair last April, we were here melting pewter and doing sand casting in the garden. Girls with gas masks.'
Faye Toogood, London. Interview by Marco Velardi. Photography by Roberta Ridolfi. 2011.

'I have the feeling I have met the last artists with what I call this form of aristocracy of the soul,
which means artists that were outside the system, or at least with a form of resistance.'
Jean-Charles de Castelbajac, Paris. Interview by Jessica Piersanti. Photography by Quentin de Briey. 2014.

'Then we went to see Kennedy's grave, and Jackie and the children came and lay flowers on it. My mother was really impressed. I didn't know that it was a big deal, because, you know, we lived in Baltimore, and I just went to Washington in a little blue suit.' Joseph Holtzman, Valatie. Interview by Sabrina Tarasoff. Photography by Todd Oldham. 2017.

'In all the houses I've ever lived in since I was small, the ground floor has always been a deposit, a studio, a warehouse. A place where, if you wanted to, you could pour paint on the floor, or throw things there, a dirty place for trying things out.' Luna Paiva & Leandro Erlich, Buenos Aires. Interview by Juan Ignacio Moralejo. Photography by Ana Armendariz. 2010.

'When I signed the lease it was a mess and I was broke. That made renovation slow and difficult.
I remember a friend of mine came to visit and she left crying.'
Marcelo Krasilcic, New York City. Interview by Michael Bullock. Photography by Marcelo Krasilcic. 2011.

Opposite: 'Sculpture, furniture—in my head, they're the same thing.'
Andrea Zittel, Joshua Tree. Interview by Alix Browne. Photography by Ryan Lowry. 2016.

...with the sky, and to bring the outside inside. The thing is that it's quite hard to train a dog, to do house training.
...to tell him or her that "this is outside, this is inside, you can pee here".'
Apichatpong Weerasethakul, Mae Rim. Interview and photography by Jeremy Liebman. 2013.

Andrea Zittel, Joshua Tree. Interview by Alix Browne. Photography by Ryan Lowry. 2016.

Opposite: 'Here everything was, and basically still is, difficult. Up to a few years ago the water was just rainwater, there was neither electric light nor even a pier where ships could dock.'
Maria Vittoria & Giorgio Backhaus, Filicudi. Text by Giorgio Backhaus. Photography by Maria Vittoria Backhaus. 2010.

'The goal of design is also coming up with a poetic object, a friendly object in the sense that it can be loved.
In Pantelleria we decided on the look of a ruin, and it is not at all in contradiction with the function.'
Oscar Tusquets Blanca, Pantelleria. Interview by Arquitectura-G. Photography by Oscar Tusquets Blanca & Lluís Clotet. 2014.

Opposite: 'He placed a lot of importance on his bathrooms ... They had to be extremely intimate spaces in which you felt relaxed,
and where you had time to think. In many ways, a place in which you could isolate yourself.'
Feature on César Manrique, Lanzarote. Interview with José Juan Ramírez, by Arquitectura-G. Photography by Nacho Alegre. 2015.

'I can't deny that I'm a voyeur, a peeping Tom. I want to know what the rich and famous live like, so I go above the wall and I look.'
Dominique Nabokov, 2010. Interview by Anja Aronowsky Cronberg. Photography by Dominique Nabokov:
Alberto Sorbelli's living room, Paris, 2000, from *Paris Living Rooms*.

Opposite: 'The winter of 1993 I was invited by Julian and Olatz Schnabel to spend some time with them in Palm Beach and New York.
There was where Julian saw my watercolours in my travelling diaries for the first time and pushed me to make them bigger and out of the diaries.'
Julian Schnabel's room corner, New York City, 1993. Text and painting by Grillo Demo. 2009.

'We do have the freaks—one couple, for example, always walk around in military attire—and the minor problems,
like someone who lets the air out of our bicycle tires or turns the washing machine to 90°, making all your clothes shrink.'
Shirana Shahbazi, Zurich. Interview by Daniel Morgenthaler. Photography by Lukas Wassmann. 2015.

Maria Vittoria & Giorgio Backhaus, Filicudi. Text by Giorgio Backhaus. Photography by Maria Vittoria Backhaus. 2010.

'I had this desire to do something by myself, but whenever I'd start to draw I'd get discouraged very fast. So this idea of drawing in the dark and not being able to see what I was drawing until it was finished came in perfectly.'
Linus Bill, Bienne. Interview and photography by Nacho Alegre. 2015.

Paulo César Pereio, São Paulo. Text by Alexandre Fehr. Photography by Richard Jensen. 2009.

Gene Krell, Tokyo. Interview by Jim Walrod. Photography by Jeremy Liebman. 2015.

'"But I have heard", says Mnauar, enriching our perspectives, "That there is a landfill in the city where people dump furniture gathered from houses facing demolition and old hotels".'
Adel Husni Bey & Mirella Clemencigh, Benghazi. Text by Mirella Clemencigh. Photography by Delfino Sisto Legnani. 2014.

'As a kid growing up, your house defines what a house is, and coming to grips with the fact that other people live
in structures that are radically different from yours takes time.'
Feature on Philolaos, Saint-Rémy-lès-Chevreuse. Interview with Marina Tloupas, by Yorgo Tloupas. Photography by Frederike Helwig. 2015.

'The process of transforming the house was also a process of adapting the house for a family with two kids.
I had to adapt the sphere to a very conventional life system.'
Eduardo Longo, São Paulo. Interview by Arquitectura-G. Photography by Richard Jensen. 2012.

'Ever since I was a little girl, all I wanted was just to have a bunch of kids. I didn't even really care about the husband or a conventional marriage—although I have been married—that was never part of the package.'
Tierney Gearon, Los Angeles. Interview by Alice Cavanagh. Photography by Tierney Gearon. 2012.

'I wanted to mix everything, do the exact opposite of what they'd told me. Like using big patterns in small rooms, which they said made the room feel smaller. On the contrary, I think the room feels bigger, almost like a landscape that you can enter through the walls.'
Carl Johan de Geer, Stockholm. Interview by Helena Nilsson Strängberg.
Photography by Carl Johan de Geer. 2010.

'I would love to have cats and plants.'
Walter Pfeiffer, Zurich. Interview by Marco Velardi. Photography by Walter Pfeiffer. 2010.

Opposite: 'There's a big, 300lb amethyst by the bathtub that I got on craigslist for free from this lady who had just recently divorced her husband.
She hated him, so she was like, "If you can carry this out of my apartment, you can have it for free".'
Ryan McGinley, New York City. Interview by Hillary Navin. Photography by Petra Collins. 2015.

Rachel Korine, Nashville. Photography by Marlene Marino. 2012.

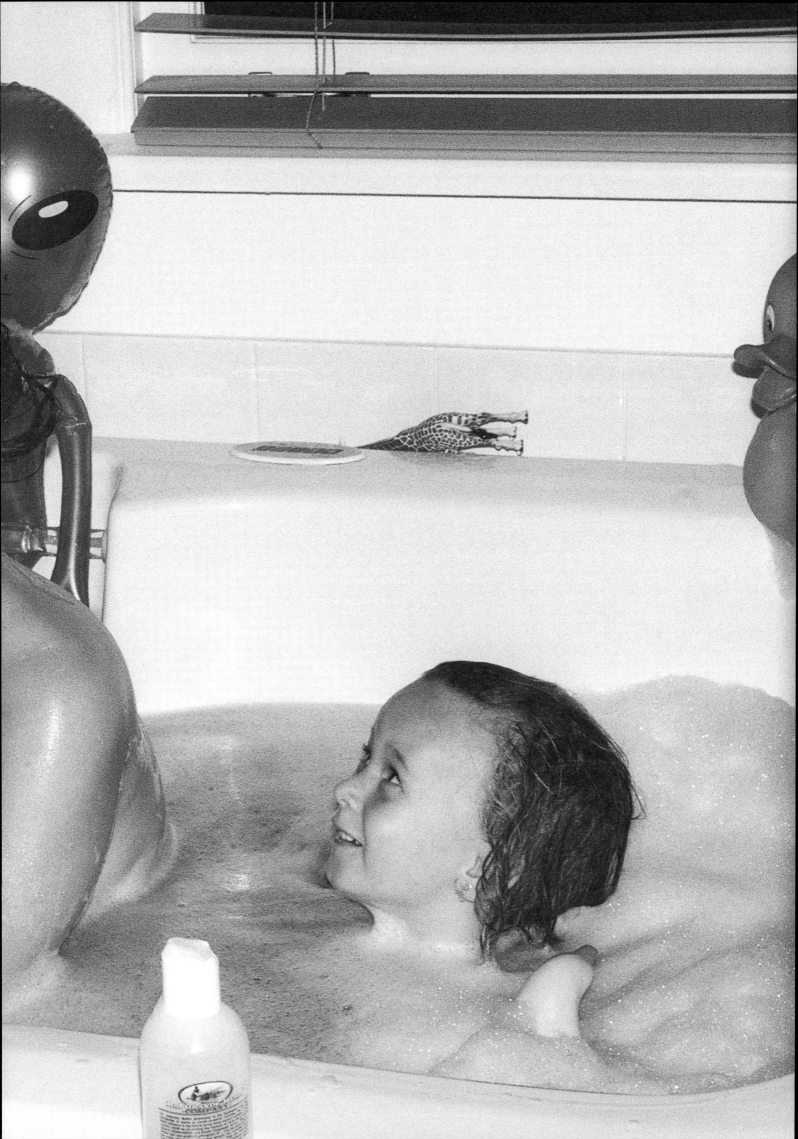

'I still wonder if you got the letter. It said, "No matter what happens between us, I will miss being here with you".'
Mỹ Linh Triệu Nguyễn, Amsterdam. Text and photography by Mỹ Linh Triệu Nguyễn. 2008.

Opposite: 'I wanted to move out of that little town where everybody knew everybody, and I was already a little bit eccentric
then so it was definitely too small a town to be eccentric in.'
Walter Pfeiffer, Zurich. Interview by Marco Velardi. Photography by Walter Pfeiffer. 2010.

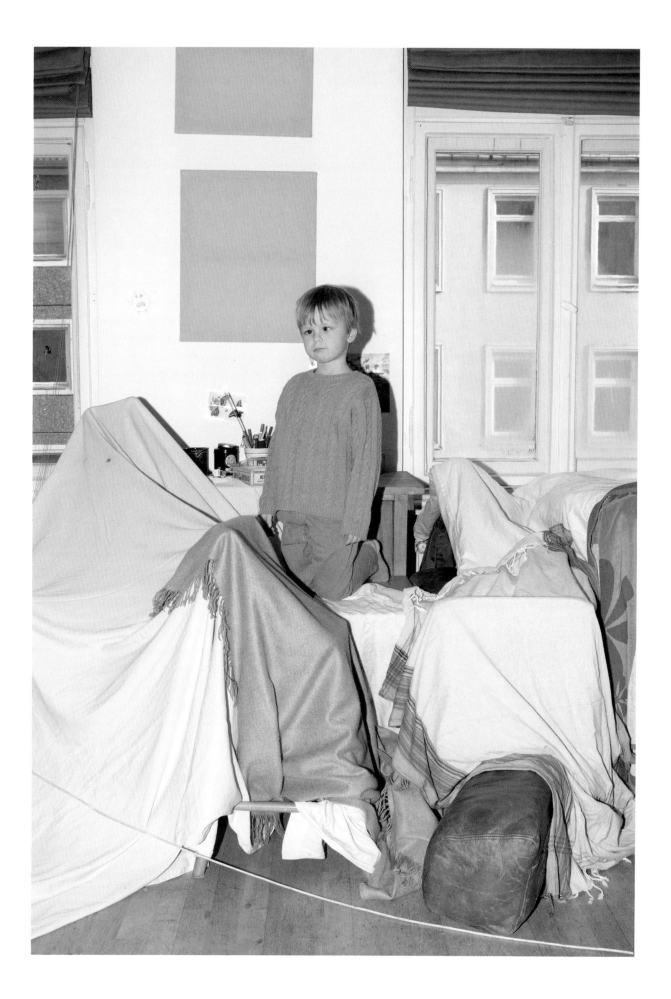

'I went over to East Berlin back then, and I almost got arrested at the border when I came back to West Berlin. I had drawn a moustache on my passport photo and the guards were very severe, they didn't believe it was me in the photo.'
Rafael Horzon, Berlin. Interview by Helena Nilsson Strängberg. Photography by Franziska Sinn. 2014.

Maria Pratts, Barcelona. Interview by Luis Cerveró. Photography by Nacho Alegre. 2017.

'We started doing some preliminary work like tearing down walls before the builders would come in. It was crazy. We would tear down one wall and behind it there was another wall with exactly the same wallpaper on it.'
Maurice Scheltens & Liesbeth Abbenes, Amsterdam. Interview by Mo Veld. Photography by Jaap Scheeren. 2013.

TAKORADI HARBO

'There was always like $50,000 in my shoe or something like that. I would usually hit my head or carry some object
so they would start focusing on something other than my smuggling qualities.'
Ford Wheeler, New York City. Interview by Flavin Judd. Photography by Jody Rogac. 2017.

'At some point Marco started chatting to a girl who was standing next to us in the bar; I think he was just interested in her plate of sausages, we were starving. We joined her group of friends and followed them drinking till 6am.'
Cosima Gadient, Basel. Text and photography by Nacho Alegre & Marco Velardi. 2009.

Marcelo Krasilcic, New York City. Interview by Michael Bullock. Photography by Marcelo Krasilcic. 2011.

Opposite: 'I remember thinking, "I'm an artist. I should be able to design the perfect space".'
Dike Blair, New York City. Interview by Jeff Rian. Photography by Henry Roy. 2013.

'I look at other people and they seem to be able to make dinner seamlessly, and for me making a meal is always this ordeal, and I always seem to get lost halfway through it.' Andrea Zittel, Joshua Tree. Interview by Alix Browne. Photography by Ryan Lowry. 2016.

'Apparently a famous soccer player lived here before us and did all the renovations ... I don't know his name so I'm not giving away anybody's secrets, but his wife or girlfriend lived in one of the front rooms with her own bathroom and then he lived in the back with this enormous closet. Sexually it seems suspect.'
AA Bronson, Berlin. Interview by Michael Bullock. Photography by Kuba Ryniewicz. 2015.

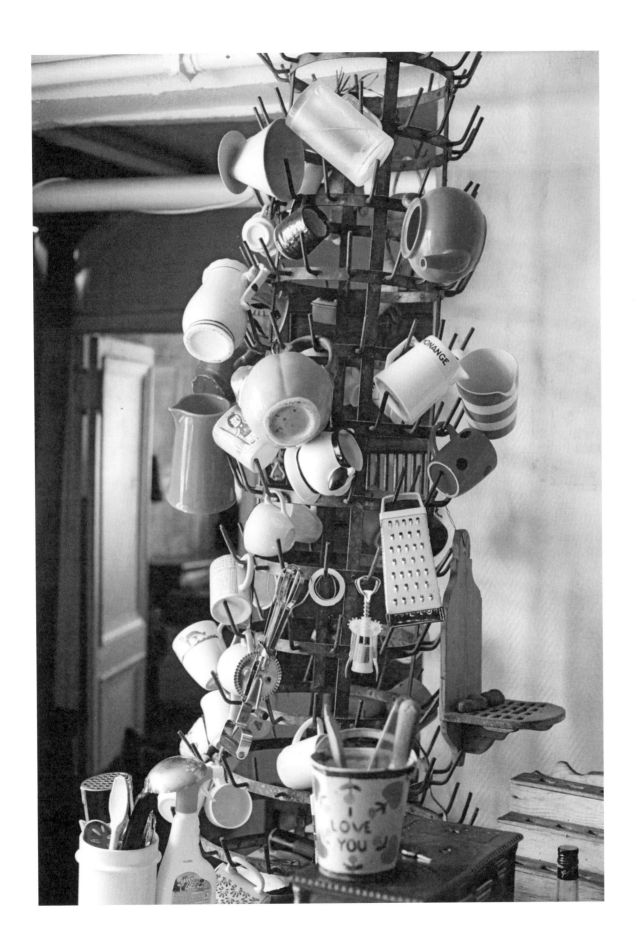

Tomás Nervi, Paris. Text and photography by Tomás Nervi. 2012.

Opposite: 'Bands would come over to get photos from me and they'd be expecting a crash pad
with posters on the wall, and they'd be like, "Whoa, what's this?"'
Edward Colver, Los Angeles. Interview by Jocko Weyland. Photography by Ramak Fazel. 2012.

'Everyone's assuming something. Nobody's actually learning anything. It's like pornography: you feel like you've got involved, but nothing's actually happened. Everyone watches the programs and absorbs their cookbooks and then they think they can cook like the chefs who wrote them.'
Margot & Fergus Henderson, London. Interview by Hugo Macdonald. Photography by Angelo Pennetta. 2017.

'Around us they are tearing down the other houses and building new, ugly ones. So it's only a matter of time before they tear down ours.'
Linus Bill, Bienne. Text and photography by Linus Bill. 2008.

Opposite: 'Now *mingei* represents this idea that nobody knows who designed something, and it changes in form slowly,
over time, out of necessity, not for stylistic reasons.'
Terry Ellis, London. Interview by Alex Tieghi-Walker. Photography by Lena C Emery. 2014.

'Shortly after we met, we wanted to realise both of our personal visions. Trix saw her house as a kind
of cavern in the ground, with a hole towards the sky. I wanted a glass tower.'
Trix & Robert Haussmann, Zurich. Interview by Daniel Morgenthaler. Photography by Lukas Wassmann. 2013.

'My goddaughter, whose father is from Marrakech, challenged me to be a hot dog for Halloween in Berlin.'
Michael Stipe, New York City. Text by Michael Stipe. Photography by David Belisle. 2013.

'Everybody says that when having kids, they need so much time and everything changes. It's true, but I think what changes the most is your relationship
with your girlfriend. Before, it was just the two of you, and that changes much more than how the kids change you.'
Linus Bill, Bienne. Interview and photography by Nacho Alegre. 2015.

TWININGS
INFUSIONS
LEMON
& GINGER

SUA MACELLERIA. ECCELLENTE NEL
CARNE E OLTRE

THINGS TO DO TODAY

'When they used to go for lunch I would go to where they were painting and paint as well.
I thought I'd done something beautiful, but when they came back they said, "Esther! What have you made here?"'
Esther Mahlangu, Weltevreden. Interview by Matthew Freemantle. Photography by Nico Krijno. 2012.

Opposite: 'The fish are great, particularly at sunset. They represent a kind of dolce vita and make summer last a little bit longer.
Maybe I'll put them in the basement this winter.'
Beda Achermann, Zurich. Interview by David Torcasso. Photography by Walter Pfeiffer. 2011.

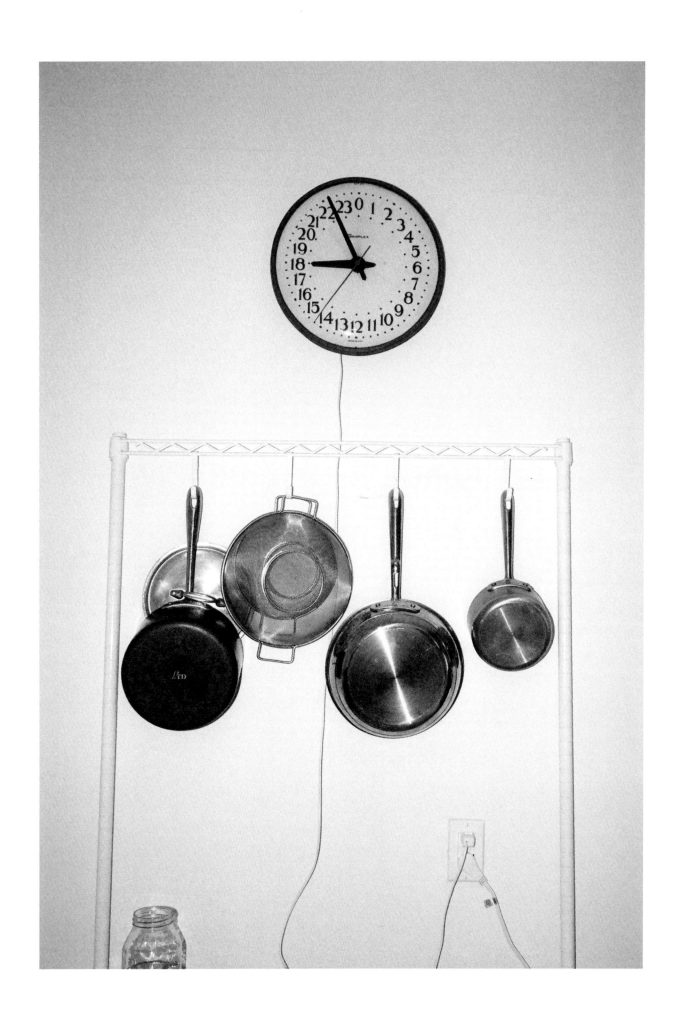

'The problem is that I feel great at four in the morning. I can just keep going and in the moment I lack the foresight
that I'm going to feel really bad the next day. So my curfew for leaving the studio is 3am.'
Tauba Auerbach, New York City. Interview and photography by Luiza Sá. 2012.

'He was very careful about how the place looked. He said once that his workshop was like his portrait and that for interviews there was no need to have a picture of him—the house, objects, and sculptures said enough.'
Feature on Philolaos, Saint-Rémy-lès-Chevreuse. Interview with Marina Tloupas, by Yorgo Tloupas. Photography by Frederike Helwig. 2015

'I've been banned by my wife from doing DIY now. I nearly killed myself about three years ago. I was trying to instal coathangers and I was drilling into the wall below the electricity fuse board.'
Erol Alkan, London. Interview by Karley Sciortino. Photography by Nacho Alegre. 2008.

'Van Chrome was an alter ego of mine who made house calls and customised people's appliances for a fee.'
Kenny Scharf, Los Angeles. Interview by Francesco Spampinato. Photography by Ye Rin Mok. 2011.

'You know how when you live in Seoul for a long time, you lose your sense of leisure?
It feels like a moment when I need some European languor.'
Na Kim, Seoul. Interview by Jae Seok Kim. Photography by Hasisi Park. 2017.

She's Taking Everything, a comic by Andy Rementer & Margherita Urbani. 2012.

the world
of apartamento

the world of apartamento
ten years of everyday life interiors

Abrams, New York

Ten years is not perhaps a long time in life, but in the recent history of magazine publishing it is a lifetime. The landscape for publishers in 2008 was very different; websites were providing competition, but the first Apple iPhone had only just arrived, and the iPad was still two years away. Facebook and Twitter existed but were minority interests.

Yet even without the subsequent digital and social media expansion, the magazine industry was well into its contemporary era of panic, as the big publishers began to acknowledge their profits and readerships were evaporating. All magazines, all at the same time, had spent decades courting seemingly ever-growing mass audiences, but it was becoming clear that the linking power of reader–magazine loyalty had been forgotten. Magazines had become commodities, with too many similar publications chasing the same people. It was all about reach instead of engagement.

Five years earlier I had published my book *magCulture: New Magazine Design*, in which it was noted that a new generation of small magazines—we termed them 'microzines'—was responding to their disappointment at what was even then happening to the big magazines. Their publishers referred to *The Face*, the *New Yorker*, and *National Geographic* as their inspiration, even though they could not possibly compete with the scale of such publications.

For these small publishers it was a matter of ambition to attempt to reach the heights of those famous magazines, to stretch for the sheer quality and relevance they found in them. Instead of focus group–tested box-ticking, they sought a better reflection of the world as they saw it. Many were super niche, and one such niche that the book identified included magazines that questioned what a magazine could/should be.

My favourite of these remains *Nice Magazine*. An A4 publication with a smart logo and a stylish advertisement on the back cover, *Nice Magazine* gave the initial impression of being a printed magazine. In fact, it was just a single block of wood cut to mimic the format of a paper magazine. It reminded the reader—if that's the correct word in this context—of the essential *physical* quality of the magazine format. That such a situationist, art-prank approach could be applied to the humble magazine seemed to me proof that there was life in the medium despite its troubles. And so it was to be.

The year 2005 saw the arrival of *Fantastic Man*, which itself had grown from another challenge to the magazine format called *Re–*, while in Berlin the anarchic newspaper *032c* was about to morph into a glossy magazine. Meanwhile, an editor, art director, and photographer working remotely in different European cities took a year to produce the first edition of their new magazine.

For its three makers, Marco, Omar, and Nacho,

Ten years of enjoyment

The cover image of *Apartamento*
magazine issue 1, featuring Joerg Koch's
apartment, Berlin, 2008.
Photography by Marco Velardi.

it wasn't until the fourth issue that they felt their magazine, *Apartamento*, had hit its stride. But as a reader coming fresh to it I can still recall that first issue as an important milestone. The shock of the empty, messy room on the cover set the tone for everything the team has done since, the randomly cropped image with a pile of discarded magazines strewn across the floor a familiar sight in real life but *never* on a front cover. And that was the point.

Apartamento set out to depict real life instead of the over-styled fakery of every other interiors magazine. The new magazine showed every bit of mess, turning away from the need to present saleable products to attract advertising and instead showing the way young people lived in their apartments. Marks were left on walls, the door to the hallway was left hanging open, and the half-finished bottle of water remained on the coffee table. If that sounds like their aesthetic grew from the grunge styling of the preceding decade, an important distinction is that *Apartamento* didn't overload the reality. It wasn't exaggerating to make a point, it was just reflecting real living. And sometimes reality could be glamorous.

The magazine, like its team, has grown up in the 10 years and 20 issues since its inception. There are a few more famous names among the interviews and apartment shoots, but it remains the same magazine in the sense that you can tell it remains a highly enjoyable project for the three principals and their small team of colleagues. Like all publishers that care, they still agonise over the details; I recall sitting with Omar after a talk in Singapore as he worried over a potential cover image, almost willing the thoroughly inappropriate picture to work.

But the way they regularly add new elements (the colour palette going ever crazier, the occasional piece of fiction), even as other things stay the course (the limited font selection, Andy Rementer and Margherita Urbani's comic stories, and Omar, Ana Domínguez, and Nacho's still life series), shows how *Apartamento*'s aesthetic is more a state of mind than a set of rigid rules. It is this that helps *Apartamento* stand apart from the many other indies that have launched in its wake. It alone is not responsible for the growth in independent magazines of the last ten years, but it has been hugely inspirational on the scene. I can think of no other recent magazine that is so loved and anticipated, so it's no surprise that today's young publishers add it to *The Face*, the *New Yorker*, and *National Geographic* as their benchmark of quality.

I'm intrigued to see where *Apartamento* gets to in another ten years!

Jeremy Leslie is the London-based authority behind magCulture, which now encompasses a design studio, journal, and shop all focused on his love of magazines.

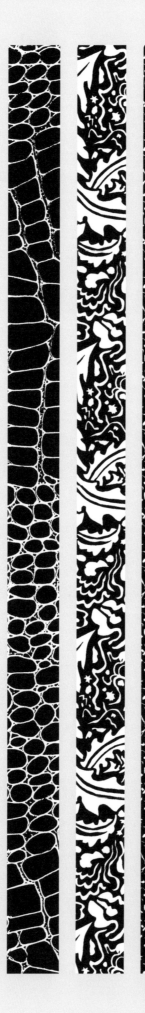

apartamento. an everyday life interiors magazine – issue #01

apartamento. an everyday life interiors magazine – issue #02

apartamento. an everyday life interiors magazine – issue #03

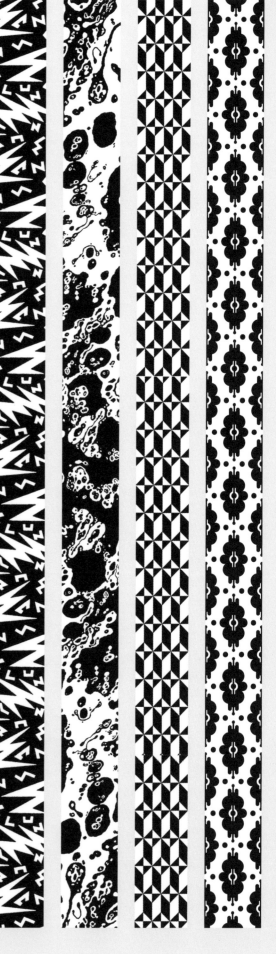

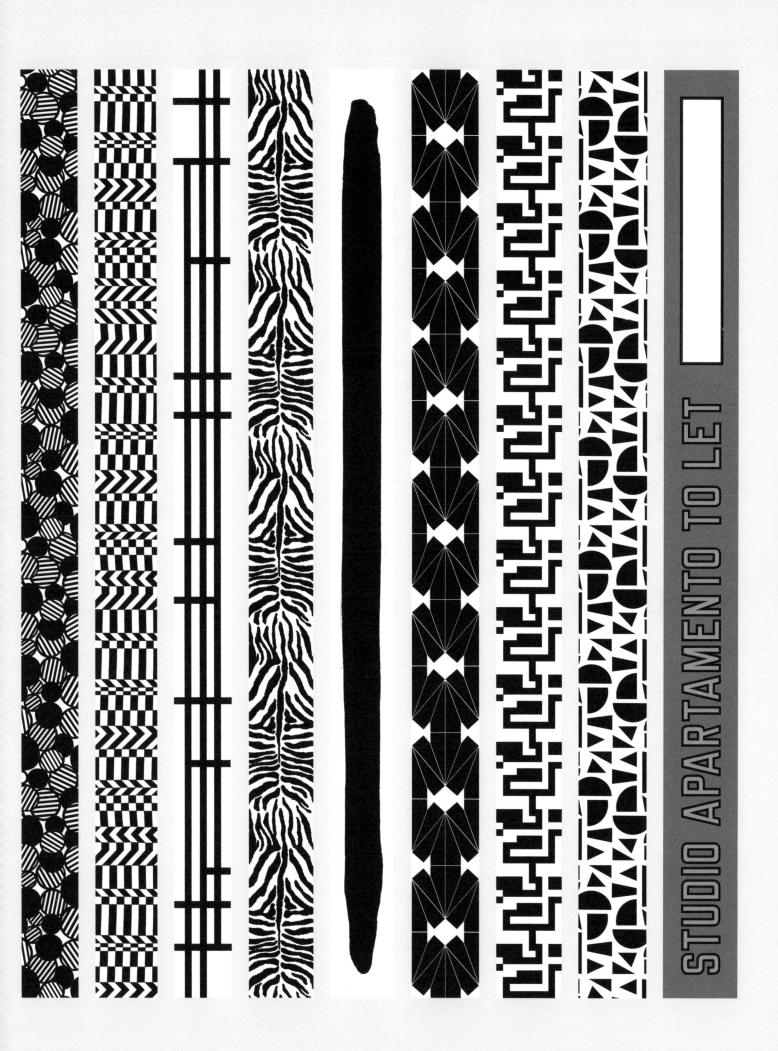

STUDIO APARTAMENTO TO LET

Apartamento spines, issues 1–20.

In Barcelona in the fall of 2006 an unimaginable magazine was born. Three young men realised that they shared an aesthetic sensibility, an enormous curiosity about how people live, and a notion that the world that excited them was nowhere to be found in their current media landscape. So, with equal parts great ambition and great naïveté, the new acquaintances Omar Sosa, Nacho Alegre, and Marco Velardi became creative collaborators and business partners. Together they invented a new type of publication, which they named *Apartamento*, adding the curious tag line 'an everyday life interiors magazine'. A wink that let you know this wasn't about the day you got your place presentable for guests, a dinner party, or a photoshoot, but all the rest of the messy, beautiful, and boring days in-between. How your life is lived when no one else is watching.

Why unimaginable? From its inception, *Apartamento* was at odds with dominant cultural clichés. First there was the incorrect but widely held assumption that architecture and design were macho fields, while homemaking and decorating were historically considered either female territory or the realm of gay men. A cliché that often stifled straight men who engaged in conversations and activities regarding home design. Incorrect because throughout history multitudes of straight men, architects like Le Corbusier and Frank Lloyd Wright, and interior designers like David Hick and Tony Duquette, and the media mogul Hugh Hefner (inventor of the bachelor pad) made spectacular contributions to our collective conception of what the inside of our homes could look like. Even so, the commercialisation of interior design, the media, and the marketing around it were often directed at female audiences. The founders of *Apartamento* were young heterosexual men in their early 20s. Omar first had the idea that there was something to add to this category when he was looking at raw spaces in Barcelona. He scanned all the available interior-design media to try and find an inspiring vision for what he should do with his own apartment and saw nothing that spoke to him, his age, his taste, or his budget. He mentioned his dismay to Nacho and found out that the latter shared the same feeling and had already been experimenting with new documentary-style formats of photographing interiors. Being outsiders to a world they were intrigued by allowed them to approach the subject of interiors from an inventive, fresh vantage point: as anthropologists instead of 'taste makers'. Instead of subscribing to

the industry's hierarchical divides along the lines of gender and sexuality, *Apartamento* presented all aspects of inhabiting space, from decorating to design, to a conscious lack of decorating and design, with equal respect and curiosity.

Marco explains their starting point: 'In the beginning we'd always just stayed in our friends' houses or on their couches, and that was the way we did it when we travelled. Maybe we've upgraded ourselves a little since then, but we've always been "parasites". It was important to do that because we were fascinated by the different spaces we'd end up in. And the thing that brought us together was the imagery of those places. It's an exploration of spending time with other people at their houses and looking at how they live. Maybe we're voyeurs more than parasites. There's some perversion in there, too'. The second widely believed notion at that moment was that print was dead, that the internet had replaced it, and that it would no longer be useful to our contemporary world. The trio ignored this warning completely. They focused on the old-fashioned medium, propelled by a desire to make a mark on a field that had given each of them pleasure, knowledge, and inspiration. Omar cites *Casa Vogue,* the work of Gert Jonkers and Jop van Bennekom (*Butt, Fantastic Man),* and the gold standard of alternative interiors magazines—Joseph Holtzman's *Nest*—as important early influences. But whether by accident or design, the printed magazine became a key tool of *Apartamento*'s success. Since their publication focused on the objects inside a home, it was important that the physical magazine could coexist with those objects in the homes of their readers. As *Apartamento* opened the conversation about interiors to an unrecognised audience, having copies of the magazine in your space signified your membership to an emerging global community—a marker of a shared post-materialist worldview.

But the most significant cliché that they casually disarmed, the radical position that set their project apart from all others in the category at that time (and perhaps the reason why you have bought this book 10 years after the first issue was printed) was the trio's unique relationship to consumerism and status. Aside from a few ground-breaking publications such as *Nest*, interior design had been almost entirely the domain of the wealthy, and the design media's job was typically to report on capitalism's biggest winners and their prizes—the celebrated architect and interior designer, designing the trophy house,

Omar and Nacho at Matter. New York, 2008.

Foodmarketo. Milan, 2010.

Launch of issue 1 at Spotti. Milan, 2008.

Everyday Life Objects Shop.
Milan, 2009.

Marco making pasta.
Foodmarketo, Milan 2010.

Launch event of issue 1 at Vinçon.
Barcelona, 2008.

Issue 0 of *Apartamento*. Barcelona, 2007.

Dinner at Nathalie Du Pasquier's home. Milan, 2011.

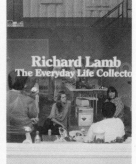

Richard Lamb, *The
Everyday Life Collectors*.
London, 2009.

Justin Bond singing at Tasca.
Ed Varie, New York, 2008

Max at the Everyday Life Objects
Shop. Milan, 2009.

Omar cooking at *Tasca Everyday Life Recipes*.
Tokyo, 2009.

Nacho's old apartment.
Barcelona, 2008.

Robbie still asleep after a long night
at Salone. Milan, 2010.

Arquitectura for kids. Milan, 2011.

Nathalie Du Pasquier and George Sowden
setting the table for a dinner in Milan, 2011.

Tasca Everyday Life Recipes.
Tokyo, 2009.

Door at the Everyday Life Objects
Shop. Milan, 2009.

filled with fashionable furniture. This approach is a powerful generator of aspiration, making it a key tool for advertisers, a system that had become so dominant that it almost blocked any other possibility. This of course was nothing new; already in 1840, Edgar Allan Poe had offered a withering critique of 'the corruption of taste' in his famous essay 'The Philosophy of Furniture': 'The cost of an article of furniture has, at length, come to be, with us, nearly the sole test of its merit in a decorative point of view ... There could be scarcely any thing more directly offensive to the eye of an artist than the interior of what is termed, in the United States, a well furnished apartment ... Undue precision spoils the appearance of many a room'.

It's true, the best that money can buy is and always will be subject to mass fascination. There is no denying that the spectacle, whether vulgar or beautiful, is dazzling, fun, and sometimes even inspiring. The images of perfection that dominate the design and lifestyle media are often so pristine that human life itself looks unwelcome. The endgame has nothing to do with the actual life lived. So, if the moneyed life is dominated by a monotone pursuit of perfection, what are the life goals of the creative community? How do painters, sculptors, photographers, novelists, editors, gallerists, film directors, fashion designers, furniture makers, and musicians live, and how are their values reflected in their living environments? Although, it's important to note that this humanist, punk editorial philosophy is not anti-wealth. The only thing they are against is a lack of personal vision. Omar explains, 'We feature people in *Apartamento* that are rich. We feature people that have decorators. The mix is what creates an interesting magazine. The important thing is that everyone has a vision—that you can see the reflection of their lifestyle in their house. Some people we feature have not very attractive apartments because they don't care. They focus their energy on something else, and that is relevant for us, too; for many interiors magazines that would be a no! "OK, he's a very interesting filmmaker, but the apartment is terrible. He can't be in an interiors magazine". We do it. If we like the person's work, we don't care'. *Apartamento* became a genre-defining cultural magazine by finding the right tone to ask the right questions at the right time and then opening up its pages to like-minded contributors to answer and explore those questions collectively. By elucidating what they would like to see themselves, Marco, Nacho, and

Omar asked, first, can a lifestyle/design magazine celebrate people's creativity regardless of the size of their wallet? Second, can it showcase reality over fantasy? Third, is there another way beyond conventional status markers to assess the value of the well-lived life?

And, fourth, is there a contemporary bohemia and, if so, what does it look like?

With this starting point the trio went to work creating their first issue, and even though they have jokingly referred to their collaborative process as a 'car crash' they quickly came to understand that working as three was an important strength. On a practical level, when they started they each brought a different but essential skill set to the table: Marco's experience was in publishing, Omar worked as a graphic designer, and Nacho worked as a photographer. Combined, they had the technical know-how needed to bring their vision into reality. But even more essential to their long-term success was the micro democracy's editorial-approval process. In their system all stories, formats, and ideas had to be signed off by all three partners. Having to win each other's approval brought an even higher level of conviction to every detail. 'The truth is we used to fight all the time. The hours we've spent fighting over the years has been a lot of hours, and that's what creates the magazine. That fight, those differences, and then the willingness to trust each other', Omar explains.

And besides having three times the passion, with an editorial board that is two parts Spanish and one part Italian, the other key by-product of having three editors is a much wider pool of curiosity. The trio is sceptical of calling themselves curators because it implies a studied, comprehensive knowledge of each creative discipline before electing each profile; this is not how they work. Their selection process is based entirely on personal interest, a gut intuition; they are making the magazine they would like to read themselves. But their selection is the extent of their presence in the magazine. 'The thing with *Apartamento* is you never hear our voice or see our face', Nacho explains. 'I think that is one of the key elements and maybe why people relate to it. In most other magazines you hear the voice of the editor, somebody's opinion; there is nothing like that behind our magazine. We don't point out things to buy. We have nothing to do with that, and I think that's important'. As editors, the trio has spoken directly to the reader only three times. In the first issue they defined their succinct but flexible mission, stating that the magazine would celebrate 'the domestic, the special, the ordinary and the not-so-ordinary, the unfinished and the personal, the austere and the baroque, the imaginary and the tangible'. But what really illuminated these concepts was their first cover. The image showed a tightly cropped sliver of an anonymous living room, the corner of a navy-blue sofa, half a grey pillow, the space is covered in piles of paper, and hundreds of different types of magazines are scattered about. 'The cover of issue 1 was like a manifesto!' Marco exclaims. 'It was really like the darkest, dirtiest, and least quality image that we could find, but we fell in love with it, it was so punk! I wouldn't choose it now, but to choose such a bad image, I think it is fantastic for an issue 1. It was a declaration: we want a mess! We want real interiors!' Magazine shops had a different take: they found its raw sensibility to be vulgar and unsellable. The trio often had to personally beg store owners to even put the first issue out on the shelf. But once they did, the jarring, rule-breaking originality of the cover helped to quickly sell out the first 5,000 copies. The other rare thing about the design and conceptualisation of the first issue was that issue 1 arrived fully formed. The different sections—the features, the ephemeral still lifes, the architectural essays by Arquitectura-G, the scale and format of the layouts, the choice of fonts, and vérité style of photography—were all clearly defined in the first issue. 'I always refer to *National Geographic*', Omar says. 'I never wanted to be too radical with the design, because for me it's about content and not about design. Everything is designed to be pleasant to read and cheap to print. But, also, I have limited time to make the magazine and I would rather put my effort into choosing the images to tell the right story. Then inventing new layouts. So it's like *National Geographic* in terms of how little the format has changed over the years'. This consistency is all in support of the main event: the personalities. Nacho goes further: 'What is special for us is the biographies. My view is that it has become for us a way to learn how to grow through the stories of other people who have succeeded in their lives. Not necessarily stories of success in regard to money or fame or commercial success, but in things we admire. It's about thinking, "How do I want my life to go, how do I want to be when I'm 60?"' Their subjects' approach to life is succinctly summed up by the late, great writer, New York City legend, and former collaborator, Glenn O'Brien: 'Style is what makes you different to others. Fashion is what makes you the same. I think it's very important not to be fashionable'. It's an ironic quirk of *Apartamento*'s subjects that the very people who ignore the current rules of interior design often have the most impact on the future of interiors. Their homes are filled with raw ideas, invention, rough drafts that are later rendered with better materials and more precision by design professionals. The men, women, and families featured in *Apartamento* don't view lifestyle as a menu of pre-set, store-bought options; instead, for them, the style in which they live is a blank canvas that they have filled with their own manner of painting, a self-fulfilling agenda with its own specific—sometimes boring, sometimes exotic, often beautiful—results. The homes of *Apartamento*'s subjects are an honest, unselfconscious reflection of their character. They are not a product of their times; instead, their conception of how to live expands the boundaries of our times.

In their 10-year anniversary issue Marco, Omar, and Nacho took the opportunity to use their voice directly once more: 'Ten years is not such a long time, but the years between your early 20s and mid-30s compress so many of the big changes that define your life as an adult. We've grown up together, shaped each other, fought with each other, and now it's hard to imagine life without each other. The three of us but also our managing editor, Robbie Whitehead, the people that have passed through the studio over the years, our advertisers, and all the writers, photographers, illustrators, contacts, friends, friends of friends'. Through 20 issues, hundreds of special projects—gallery exhibitions, collaborations, cookbooks, children's books, gentle, unpretentious small-scale launch events that often brought people together over a home-cooked meal—this humble but sprawling project has intimately connected thousands of people across generations, disciplines, locations, and cultures, from New York City to Barcelona, from Buenos Aires to Tokyo, and everywhere in-between.

This book is a tribute to these connections, showing us visually what they have in common. It further shares the moments that tell us about how and why people who have chosen to live outside of society's conventions have achieved the life they desired. And at the end of all this, what we have collectively learned from *Apartamento* is one meaningful and comforting fact: there are no general rules for how we should inhabit our homes or live our lives.

Michael Bullock has been heavily involved in the independent magazine industry for more than a decade, and is a contributing editor to *Apartamento*. His articles revolve around the world of LGBT and outsider culture.

Enzo Mari showing us how
to open walnuts at
Foodmarketo.
Milan 2010.

Nacho and Fergus Henderson.
St. John, London, 2017.

Jeremy Liebman at issue 13
launch event, The Girards.
New York, 2014.

Ana Dominguez stocking up on chewing gum.
New York, 2009.

Max Lamb, an outtake from
the article in issue 2. London, 2008.

Jim Walrod and Patrick Parrish at Mondo
Cane's Garage Sale. New York, 2012.

Nathalie Du Pasquier's show and *Apartamento*'s Launch,
Paris 2014.

Nacho peddling copies
of issue 16 on the streets of
Milan, 2016.

Marco during party post-editorial
meeting, Barcelona, 2009.

Jasper Morrison – Outrageous acts of balance!

We've all enjoyed the childish game of making a stack out of seemingly inappropriate materials, and though it might be more for kids, it's nevertheless a lot of fun. For most of us it's an occasional pastime, but for the men at *Apartamento* it's a duty, involving serious research, lengthy shopping trips, and a studio photoshoot.

I've heard of people who spend a lot of time stacking things, but they mostly do it to achieve outrageous acts of balance and don't pay too much attention to the articles in the stack.

The *Apartamento* stackers, on the other hand, will only stack things which share a typological identity. Loaves of bread, rolls of tape, terracotta bricks, blocks of ice, lumps of clay, to name a few examples, are all subjected to an arrangement that stands precariously on a small platform between conceptual logic, absurdity, good taste, and bad taste. They ask to be taken seriously and they try to win our sympathy by being ridiculous. Salvador Dalí, Irving Penn, Claes Oldenburg, Fischli and Weiss, and Ettore Sottsass have each made guest appearances here, and it all holds together by careful arrangement. Normally there's a financial motivation for making a display, an urge to have a thing noticed and then sell it, but in this case, at the luxury end of the display business, the only motivation is to please us.

Concepts by Ana Dominguez and Omar Sosa. Photography by Nacho Alegre.

Issue 1: Porcelain; Issue 2: Fabric; Issue 3: Marble & granite;
Issue 4: Drinking glasses; Issue 5: Wood; Issue 6: Inox; Issue 7: Bricks; Issue 8: Bread;
Issue 9: Candles; Issue 10: Tape; Issue 11: Clay; Issue 12: Magnets;
Issue 13: Sugar; Issue 14: Ice; Issue 15: Brass & copper;
Issue 16: Paper; Issue 17: Foam; Issue 18: Patatas; Issue 19: Plastic bags;
Issue 20: Toilet paper

Jasper Morrison is a renowned product and furniture designer from the UK.

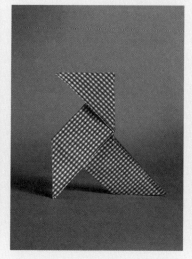

I bumped into Marco and Nacho in Basel in June 2008. As scruffy-looking and out of place as me, and with a cheeky glint in their eyes, they were endearingly wielding a copy of issue 1 of *Apartamento* while simultaneously scouting for new friends and content for their second issue. A few weeks later Marco showed up at my door in London with only a Contax camera in the pocket of his well-worn wax jacket. It wasn't a photo-shoot, more of a coffee and chat while rummaging through our home, studio, and lives. In fact, I don't think Marco even drank our coffee. Photos were obviously taken, but I don't remember this. Marco talks really quickly and changes subject multiple times in each sentence, which is an excellent distraction tactic. But the photos Marco took that day are a testament to how quickly he and Omar and Nacho become a part of the lives they celebrate. Intimacy like that can't be faked. Everyone is family. The *Apartamento* boys are a living manifesto, and their love and energy is immediately infectious. By the end of the conversation our lives had been photographed, and somehow I'd offered to design a piece of furniture especially for the second issue of *Apartamento*.

The DIY chair embodies the community spirit and generosity that Marco brought with him when he knocked on Gemma's and my front door, and what Omar wrote in his opening statement introducing issue 1 of the magazine: 'presenting interior design exactly how it is in practice'. The DIY chair was designed for everyone and anyone. It was designed to be made and made to be used, not to be observed as a design object, occupying the corner of a room. This same spirit of sharing and being 'real' is evident in every issue of *Apartamento* and every exhibition, event, and dinner they organise. Just as *Apartamento* portrays the honest everyday environments that motivated makers and creatives *actually* work and live in, as opposed to the polished and curated interiors shown in other publications, the DIY chair was designed as a template for everyday people and their everyday lives, the one caveat being they need to make it first. With this notion the DIY chair has become a metaphor for how I understand *Apartamento*; if they can do it themselves, perhaps everyone can. At least, everyone should try.

Since the DIY chair and its instructions were published in 2008 I've received, and continue to receive, dozens of photos of DIY chairs made by *Apartamento* readers and their extended family. Real chairs made by real people for use in real homes. Some take it one step further, evolving the design to become DIY stools, tables, shelving, and even lighting—exactly as I had hoped. When curators ask to borrow a DIY chair for an exhibition I tell them to make one. The DIY chair has naturally dispersed itself around the world. A few months later I found Marco sitting at the dining table eating dinner with my parents and my grandpa on his farm in Yorkshire. And so the *Apartamento* family continues to grow.

Max Lamb's DIY Chair,
designed especially for *Apartamento*
issue 2, 2008.

Max Lamb is a British designer known for his DIY mentality and fascination with processes and materials.
His work employs rudimentary methods applied in unexpected and creative ways.

Not 20 years ago, magazines were the internet and I deferred to my stack for critical guidance. There was always a stack, often out of control, and I looked forward to long flights with a heavy rucksack-full to clean things up. Upon arrival I would feel unburdened and enlightened; precious torn pages would make their way into files on every conceivable subject and destination that might someday be of interest to me—my analogue bookmarks of a bygone era. Much as the stack might have been overwhelming, the digital deluge would soon change all the rules.

It was once a point of laborious finesse to establish one's bona fides, that short list of restaurants, hotels, haberdashers, cobblers, and the like—all those obscure makers and merchants, the merchandise and places by which we define ourselves, with reasonable confidence in our singular style. In a world of abundant, accessible knowledge and wares, the art of editing oneself has become daunting. Too many choices; too many arbiters. And to further confuse matters, the entire notion of retailing has been upended and reinvented as the tightly edited temple of object worship, where one can find a bit of everything, all with the imprimatur of a celebrated eye.

The magazine world has its own rendition of this compendium of style. But whose style is this? Are these not catalogues of cliché which defy the notion of originality? Care to be a woodsman, an urban hipster, a dandy, a country gent? Go to the rack and choose your publication accordingly, and the costume, accoutrement, and related locales are only a wannabe website away. Of course, all this is proposed under the auspices of good taste, but the distinction between good taste and style is the vast differential at the root of individuality. And where to go to celebrate this most elusive of traits?

Perhaps this is the foremost cleverness of *Apartamento*: its modest physical dimensions invariably land it symbolically and deservedly atop the stack. And it is appropriately diminutive as to be well suited to its unspoken intention to act as a handbook of style, a manual of originality. Perhaps one could refer to *Apartamento* as a 'who's who of who?' I am frequently amused, surprised, and impressed by those little-known and underappreciated players in its pages, who inhabit the fringes of renown and—for the most part—thankfully seem to shun the carefully groomed showrooms surrounded by perfectly posed props, with lives devoted to the next photogenic moment.

Though all this seems so casually assembled as if to appear intentionally engineered, in fact *Apartamento* is a tactile work of alchemy, a celebration of the ordinary extraordinary.

From 1997 to 2016, Michael Maharam was CEO of Maharam, the century-old family business that has come to be known as one of the leading suppliers of textiles to architects and interior designers in the United States.

I was once asked by a friend, as a favour, if I would agree to have my home photographed by the decorating magazine for which he worked. Jean-Louis was a friend of long-standing and I said yes. On the appointed day, he and a photographer showed up at the house. I took them around the small cottage, which my wife and I had built ourselves. One wall of the compact sitting room was covered in bookshelves. There were too many books, the photographer declared, couldn't we remove some of them? I explained that I was a writer and books were a big part of my life. He looked sceptical. In addition to the usual photographic equipment, he had brought a box of what turned out to be stage props—an espresso machine, some decorative plates, a potted plant. Jean-Louis explained that these objects were needed to add interest to the photographs. I realised then that this project was not really about our home, but about fashionable appearances.

Thus, the first time I saw a copy of *Apartamento* I thought to myself, 'Oh well, another home decorating mag'. I assumed it would contain the usual voyeuristic collection of perfectly groomed interiors; I was mistaken. The staples of the so-called shelter press are rooms and furniture, and while these were present in the pages of the magazine, its real subject was not interiors but their occupants. The people who appear in *Apartamento* are unusual, you say. They are certainly a mixed bag: old and young, fashion-conscious and eccentric, disciplined and quirky, edgily urban and romantically rural, nomadic and rooted in place. Their homes reflect this heterogeneity, an eclectic mix that is more emblematic of our times than the staged interiors of the shelter press. This is how people live today.

What is interesting is not a home's décor but what it says about its occupants—the way they choose to live, their obsessions and dreams, the eccentric paraphernalia of their everyday lives. We surround ourselves with objects that are accumulated, inherited, their meanings known only to ourselves. This clutter is not stylistically consistent; it's more like a diary, a three-dimensional record of the passing years. In my home, the beat-up Aalto stools are the first pieces of furniture I ever bought for myself, the handmade Québécois rush armchair was given to me by a friend, a pair of old-fashioned wing chairs, recently re-covered, was provided by a furniture company in lieu of a lecture fee.

Architects and interior designers say that 'people occupy space', but what they really mean is that we make the space and *they* occupy it. Designed interiors have an autonomous existence. I often have the feeling that the owners are interlopers in their own homes, whose every detail has been chosen and arranged by someone else. 'We don't move anything', the occupants say proudly. 'It's like living in a work of art'. I can't imagine anything more disagreeable.

The idea that the decoration of a home requires outside expertise originated in the 18th century, when cabinetmakers and upholsterers in London and Paris emerged as the arbiters of domestic taste. They not only provided furniture to their clients but coordinated the work of various decorator craftsmen to create integrated interiors. The results were often quite beautiful, but they were not—and were not intended to be—an expression of the personality of the owner.

There is a rare exception of that period: the home that Voltaire and Émilie, the Marquise du Châtelet, created in the Château de Cirey, a crumbling old country house built in the previous century. Voltaire, whose business investments had made him wealthy, paid for a restoration. And in return, the marquise's complaisant husband, who was often away, turned a blind eye to his wife's unconventional domestic arrangement. The interior reflected the lovers' interests: hers, science; his, science and philosophy. They each had their own study packed with books, and they shared scientific equipment; Voltaire had a miniature theatre built in the attic where guests were dragooned into performing his plays.

The pair collaborated on the interior design. 'She is putting windows where I've put doors, she's changing staircases into chimneys, and chimneys into staircases', he complained. They added a new wing facing the garden. Part living room and part laboratory, this gallery was where the couple, who spent the day in solitary pursuits, met in the evenings. The yellow-panelled room was a clutter of books, telescopes, microscopes, and astronomical models, with space for her harpsichord as well as their pet parrot. Not that the décor was bohemian; the interior was the work of fashionable Parisian decorators and cabinetmakers working in high rococo style. But the result was intensely personal, an interior that mirrored the interior lives of its remarkable occupants. Voltaire and du Châtelet occupied Cirey from 1734 until her death in 1749. '*Mon paradis terrestre*', he called it.

Witold Rybczynski is emeritus professor of urbanism at the University of Pennsylvania. In addition, he's an architect and author, writing on the subjects of housing, architecture, and technology.

I first encountered *Apartamento* when I was working at *T: The New York Times Style Magazine* as the deputy design editor. Under the guidance and vision of Pilar Viladas, whose knowledge of architecture and design is encyclopaedic, *T* was publishing the sorts of stories you could not find anywhere else. Pilar seemed to be chronically allergic to decorating. Or more specifically, to houses or apartments that had been decorated impersonally and over-tastefully by a hired gun and, as a result, told you little to nothing about the people who actually lived there. At *T* we gravitated towards the eccentric, the unusual, the quirky. Yet, another of Pilar's tics was that we were never to refer to these houses and apartments as homes. So even as the houses and apartments we featured purportedly offered a window onto the people who inhabited them, we almost never invited those inhabitants to appear in our pages.

In 2010, I commissioned a story for *T* about *Apartamento* and a handful of other like-minded indie publications that were forging a brave new world of interiors. 'A-list designers like Bertjan Pot and Max Lamb show up to offer D.I.Y. projects for the particularly ambitious reader', wrote Mark Rozzo, referring to *Apartamento* specifically. '"It's not really a D.I.Y. magazine", said the Netherlands-based Pot, who created Xeroxable potato-patterned wallpaper for Issue 4. "But it says, Be happy with what you have, and if you can't buy it, you can make it yourself. It's all in your hands"'. The story, while celebrating this novel vérité approach, nevertheless questioned whether it was necessary to be subjected to someone's stack of bills, their dusty paperbacks, and their unsightly remote control. 'Yes, we wish we had a castle in the backyard, too. But this is our reality', *Apartamento*'s Marco Velardi said with an implied shrug. We called the *T* story 'How This Half Lives'. The more I got to know *Apartamento* and, more significantly, became friendly with its editors—

Marco, Omar, Nacho, and Robbie—the more I realised that I in fact aspired to belong to this half, and not the other half that populated the pages of most interiors magazines. Even as I prided myself on my burgeoning knowledge of design, and dare I say my highly original taste, I was certainly not living a life worthy of *Architectural Digest*, or for that matter *T*. Nor, to be honest, did I want to.

Here was my reality: I had just had a baby. I had just returned to work at the *Times*. I was going through an ugly break-up. Basically, my life was in a state of total turmoil—as my domestic situation so plainly broadcast. I was able to navigate this very difficult and, in retrospect, incredibly enlightening period through a series of essays I wrote for *Apartamento* starting in 2009. I spoke of clearing my ex's crap out of my apartment and reclaiming it as my own. I wrote of the challenge of sharing space with a small person who has yet to discover the concept of boundaries (eight years later she still hasn't). I wrote of the joy, however fleeting, of visiting IKEA with a toddler. Here I was, barely hanging on and self-administering my own form of apartment therapy. And so you can imagine my surprise when my unflinchingly personal essays were not only not rejected by *Apartamento*, but fully embraced and, on occasion, given pride of place on the opening pages of the magazine. I had found a home (not to be confused with a house or an apartment).

Apartamento claims to be an everyday life interiors magazine. (It says as much on the front cover of every issue.) But I would argue that said interiors are first and foremost the wonderful and incredible interior lives of the magazine's subjects, contributors, and creators. A space is interesting because of the person who inhabits it, *Apartamento* insists, and not the other way around. Life is beautiful not in spite of the fact, but ultimately because it is messy.

Alix's living room
from *Apartamento* issue 7, 2011

As well as being a contributing editor at *Apartamento*, Alix Browne is editor in residence at Helmut Lang, founding editor of *V Magazine*, former features director of *W Magazine*, and deputy design editor at *T: The New York Times Style Magazine*.

This year has been a special one for us: our studio, Arquitectura-G, turned 10 years old, an anniversary we've shared with our friends at *Apartamento*. We all met many years ago: we frequented the same places, moved in the same circles, and used any excuse as an opportunity to do something. That's how our collaboration was born, naturally, as things between friends usually do. We've gone from being 20-somethings to being 30-somethings, almost without realising. But a lot of things have changed during this time. They've seen us grow as a studio little by little. Our team has got bigger, and so has the scale of our projects. We hardly need to mention their successes; this book was born of those achievements, and this deserves to be celebrated.

Are 10 years of collaboration important in a lifetime? Yes, probably, and all the more so if we consider this collaboration as a sequence of events that have contributed to our life stories. It's not only a question of having lived through hardships and triumphs together; it's about the personal and intellectual enrichment these moments have brought us—the constant evolution that keeps us seeing things from new angles. This time has allowed us to understand the importance of certain characteristics of architecture that have directly influenced our work, and that previously went unnoticed. The most important of these is probably density, the personal stories that accompany each project, whatever the artistic discipline may be. We're most excited about architecture that possesses a special aura, that transcends form, function, or structural logic. It's what we tend to call 'ARCHITECTURE with capital letters' here in the studio, pieces that respond directly to a unique story and conceal labyrinths with infinite threads to pull on. They are projects that can be understood on different levels and can be taken as far as you want to take them.

In a way, *Apartamento* shows us these layers. Although many people misunderstand the publication as an interiors magazine, or a simple style guide for the modus vivendi of a generation, it speaks about the stories and personal histories that construct spaces. Ten years ago, while having a beer with Nacho and Omar, they told us that when they had to photograph or do the art direction for fashion editorials, they'd end up being more interested in what surrounded the models than the models themselves. They were planning to launch a magazine that talked about lived-in spaces. Their intuition showed them that the secret of the aura of the spaces we inhabit hides behind the stories that give them form. They asked us to speak about architecture from a more canonical point of view, in a section a little bit different from the rest of the magazine that would function almost as an insert.

We loved the idea and began our collaboration. We chose to talk about houses because we thought it fit with the domestic scale the magazine was going to deal with. We decided that in each issue we'd discuss one unique dwelling, holding a conversation with the project's author–architect, and on occasion we'd invite Ekhi Lopetegi, Moisés Puente, or Guillermo López as a third guest. In the initial conversations we maintained a fairly objective approach to each project, but at a certain point the more descriptive aspects were left in the background, and we focused on telling a story that went beyond the design. We've had the chance to meet incomparable characters, whose personalities are just as important and interesting as their work, where one can't be understood without delving into the other. And we've been able to share these experiences with the magazine's readers. We're interested in investigating the origin of certain decisions: not so much 'why are there three rooms in a row?' but 'why are there three rooms?' The result is that, in many issues, the texts have focused on houses that the architects have made for themselves, because these are the places where they've most clearly given form to their desires and fears.

Architecture is largely about time. It's a slow process in which many things happen between the initial sketches and the final construction of a project. But that's exactly what allows it to mix with life. Throughout the 20 issues of the magazine, our collaborations have overlapped in time with the construction of various dwellings in which Nacho, Omar, and Robbie have lived. We like to think that, in some way, they eat, sleep, cry, or laugh in places that hold part of what we are. And what we are and will be is also, in part, thanks to *Apartamento*.

Arquitectura-G is a Barcelona-based architecture studio. They were awarded the Mies van der Rohe Emerging Architect prize in 2015 and have been contributing editors to *Apartamento* since issue 1.

When the current issue of *Apartamento* arrived at our home, my wife offhandedly commented that the shelter magazines she likes best are the *World of Interiors*, a London-based Anglo-centric publication, and *Apartamento*. This surprised me because I had never thought of *Apartamento*, despite its name, as a shelter magazine. Most shelter magazines offer up the popular interior-design memes du jour, meticulously styled. Everything is made to look alluring and glamorous. Beyond their informational function, however, shelter magazines are vehicles for showing off. The photographs are meant to inspire envy. This is unkind. *Apartamento*, on the other hand, has a more humane agenda: to communicate the way creators actually live, work, and think. The environments pictured in *Apartamento* are often raw and/or messy—i.e., lived in. Fantasies of 'success' and 'achievement' are kept to a minimum so that a sense of human reality comes through. *Apartamento* hones in on people who rely more on their inventiveness than their pocketbooks. Ironically, many of the creators featured in *Apartamento* make or inspire the things that appear in the picture-perfect bourgeois palaces featured in the more conventional shelter magazines.

My wife made a valid point. *Apartamento* is a shelter magazine. But it is also something more. It is a creative-lifestyle magazine, or more precisely, an idiosyncratic creative-lifestyle magazine. I know a little about this genre because, in the dark ages before personal computers, I published a kindred publication titled *WET: The Magazine of Gourmet Bathing*. Like *Apartamento*, *WET* was a favourite of the artistic creative class of its day. During that time—the mid '70s to early '80s—publishing a print-on-paper magazine was the least expensive and most effective way to present a comprehensive aesthetic worldview to a global audience.

This may not be the case today, which prompts the question: are the costs associated with bringing a physical magazine like *Apartamento* into existence justified? For me the answer is an unequivocal yes. There is nothing like the sensorial experience of diving into a physical magazine. You can feel the energy and excitement in your hands. The ink-saturated paper images transport you in a way that images on a screen just don't. (And you can even cut them out and pin them on your actual wall!) Additionally, there is something deeply reassuring about a flexible hunk of processed-wood product lying silently present on your coffee table or on your bookshelf—a solid object that you can take comfort in, again and again and again.

By coincidence, I recently made the acquaintance of one member of the creative trio that puts *Apartamento* together. We shared a couple of stimulating dinners, a walk, and two museum visits. Omar reminded me of my younger self. He also reminded me of what it takes to make a magazine like *Apartamento*. You have to be very skilful in dealing with sensitive, creative people. You have to be diplomatic, kind, charming, and cajoling. You also have to be firm, because sometimes you have to say no—even at the risk of hurting someone's feelings. And you have to be very disciplined, because you are always working with deadlines. I was also reminded that the makers of exciting magazines like *Apartamento* are very curious people. They know how to smell an intriguing story. They have faith that what is interesting to them will be of interest to others. They have a sense of balance, because a magazine with only one flavour is boring. And, like good (figurative) chefs, they are able to bring their magazine to the cultural table imaginatively seasoned and chock-full of piping-hot relevance.

Leonard Koren is an American artist, author of *Wabi-Sabi for Artists, Designers, Poets & Philosophers*, and founder/editor of *WET: The Magazine of Gourmet Bathing*.

First of all, *Apartamento* must be pronounced with a Spanish accent.

Apartamento is not always an *apartamento*; sometimes it's a big house, sometimes it's in a desert, sometimes in an old building, sometimes in a new one. Sometimes it is the home of old people, sometimes young people. Sometimes people live there alone, sometimes with someone else or a family or a dog or a rabbit. The inhabitants of these *apartamentos* are mostly 'interesting' people.

There are always things in a home, and the things you live with reveal a lot about who you are and in what time you live; they follow trends, like in fashion, but also identify you in a way you are not always conscious of. The homes of older people tend to present an accumulation of all that has been achieved. The homes of younger people are, of course, more related to the trends of the moment. The photos of these interiors are purposely 'not beautiful'. They tend to be a bit indiscreet. There are close-ups of details—the books in disorder on the table, the dirty plates— as if the interviewer was more a friend of the person interviewed than a journalist. And, in fact, the interviewer is not a journalist; *Apartamento* is about meeting people at home. And these people are part of a strange international network, friends of friends of friends.

The magazine is an anthropological document about the tribe of the 'cool'. Sometimes *Apartamento* gets on my nerves. Sometimes the interviews are very interesting and you would like to meet the people, and sometimes not at all; it's normal that when you meet people, you don't like them all.

Then there is a section that seems to have nothing to do with the magazine: a few pages of abstract poetry, little compositions arranged by Omar Sosa and Ana Domínguez and photographed by Nacho Alegre. There are no words, no people, the constructions are totally ephemeral, you know the elements will go back to where they belong as soon as the photos are done. I very much like that section. Sometimes there is also a comic strip I love by Andy Rementer and Margherita Urbani; it's about what happens in homes, simple unhappy things which have to do with love and how all our possessions testify to our melancholy. There is a strange contrast between these stories, where the characters are just very normal, simple animals, and the rest of the magazine, where everything seems so special and great.

One more nice thing about *Apartamento*: it is not about news. You can enjoy the magazine even years after it came out. This morning, for example, I took out an old issue and read a story that had no photos, a story of a young man in Beijing who meets some Chinese businesspeople who propose that he act as an American architect in order to convince some big clients to build a shopping mall. A very Chinese story. My boyfriend is in China at the moment, and the story is so well told it made me feel I was in China, too—out of my *apartamento*!

A drawing by Nathalie Du Pasquier
celebrating the release of
Apartamento issue 10.

The French-born artist and designer Nathalie Du Pasquier has lived in Milan since 1979.
Nathalie was one of the founding members of the Ettore Sottsass-led Memphis design collective

I have a distinct memory of my first encounter with *Apartamento*, and that's something I cannot say of any other magazine. I was in Lisbon for a meeting related to the now defunct design biennial Experimenta. We were lunching on a sunny terrace overlooking the city and I happened to sit next to Marco Velardi. He showed me a copy of issue 1, and I was immediately taken. An interiors magazine for people who sleep on each other's sofas! It was surprisingly radical and absolutely timely. I said as much, and Marco gave me the copy for keeps.

On its launch, *Apartamento* existed in relation to a triangle of existing publications. Most obviously, it felt like a retort to *Wallpaper**, which had been launched just over a decade earlier by Tyler Brûlé. An impregnable universe of white B&B Italia corner sofas and Scandi-modern styling, that publication had appeared fully fledged at birth in a way that was at once beguiling and infuriating. I was teaching at the Royal College of Art in 1997 and invited Brûlé to speak to my students. As he entered the lecture theatre they were baying for his blood, but by the time he left they were eating out of his hand. But Brûlé had left in 2002, and *Wallpaper** had faltered. A decade on from its debut, the magazine's use of the editorial 'we' had lost its cheerily arch quality and become strained.

Then there was the *World of Interiors,* which had developed a brilliant stride under founding editor Min Hogg between 1981 and 2001. By 2007, although still churning out images of fabulous interiors, it had become a touch formulaic. From my position on the Portuguese terrace, the most apt comparison seemed to be *Nest*, a magazine that ran for 26 issues between 1997 and 2004, edited and designed by the singular Joseph Holtzman. Encompassing prison cells, igloos, and actual nests, Holtzman had expanded the discussion of domesticity. Strange to remember it now, but in the mid '90s we were all in the grips of doctrinaire aesthetic minimalism, a condition outlined in John Pawson's 1996 book, *Minimum*. In that light, *Nest*'s embrace of riotous colour and decoration had come as a relief.

The responsibility of breaking the stranglehold of restraint seems to have proved too much for Holtzman, however. He wrote one of his editor's letters from what he described as a 'small, well-proportioned room' in a psychiatric hospital. Once *Nest*

disappeared in 2004, all we were left with was the increasingly rigid aristocratic historicism of *World of Interiors* and *Wallpaper**'s ever blander bachelor-pad iterations of Pawson. They were aesthetically straitened times. Enter *Apartamento* and its championing of 'everyday life interiors'.

For the past 10 years I have followed the magazine as an occasional contributor and consistent reader. I still scour its images for unexpected details and its interviews for unguarded remarks, but where once it seemed absolutely of the moment, even slightly ahead of its time, now it has become almost nostalgic. In 2008 the idea of domestic space as a flexible makeshift quantity seemed radical, but a decade later the concept of domesticity of any kind has begun to appear as a thing of the past.

This development is tied up with circumstances that have allowed Airbnb to thrive. Launched a neatly coincidental decade ago in San Francisco, the website was initially envisaged as a vehicle through which hosts could make extra money by accommodating paying guests in spare space. Immediately appearing ideologically and aesthetically aligned to *Apartamento*, Airbnb's vibe has changed significantly over the last 10 years. Now, rather than bedding down on air mattresses in communal living spaces, the trend is for Airbnb guests to be staying in generic buy-to-let properties. Sharing has made way for the monopolising means and the maximising profits.

And here we are in 2018. Young people can no longer afford to buy or even rent homes in major cities and the digitally enabled movement from one soulless rented space to another has become ceaseless. The model proposed by the artist Christopher Kulendran Thomas, in which you subscribe to a 'home' that can exist in several cities with all the domesticity you might require being downloadable from the cloud, seems near at hand. Depending on your point of view, this vision might be heaven or hell, but, regardless of your take, if everyone started to live like that, there would be no more *Apartamento*. In the universe of domestic subscriptions, specificity would only exist in the realm of communications and entertainment.

From a sunny terrace in Lisbon, I end with an apocalyptic conclusion. *Apartamento*'s rich and particular environments might be endangered, so let's enjoy them while they last!

Emily King is a London-based design historian who concentrates on writing and curating. She's also a contributing editor to *Apartamento, Frieze,* and *The Gentlewoman*.

Covers

Issue 1
Spring/Summer 2008
Featuring: Aya Yamamoto, Benjamin, Sommerhalder, Elein Fleiss, Giacomo De Poli, Gunnar Knechtel, Hugo de la Rosa, Laboratorium, Linus Bill, Luiza Sá, Martino Gamper, Mike Mills, Mystery Jets, Nolaster, Skye Parrott, Paul Schiek.

Issue 2
Autumn/Winter 2008-09
Featuring: Carlotta Manaigo, Christopher Bollen, Erol Alkan, FAR, Felix Friedmann, Julian Gatto, Markus Miessen, Mathias Sterner, Max Lamb, Mylinh Trieu Nguyen, Terence Koh, Wai Lin Tse, Ye Rin Mok, Yorgo Tloupas.

Issue 3
Spring/Summer 2009
Featuring: Alexandrea Singh, David Armstrong, Ezra Koenig, JD Samson, Jean Touitou, Juan Tessi, Nakameguro, Paulo Cesar Pereio, Powerhouse Company.

Issue 4
Autumn/Winter 2009-10
Featuring: Andy Rementer, Bertjan Pot, Chloë Sevigny, Cyril Duval, Enzo Mari, Grillo Demo, Gustavo Di Mario, Mark & Garrick, Philip Crangi, Sonic Youth, Sonya Park, Stella Sabin, Tatiana Bilbao.

Issue 5
Spring/Summer 2010
Featuring: Alex Wiederin, Daniel Riera, Dominique Nabokov, Imaad Wasif, Justin Bond, Lovefoxxx, Luna & Leandro, Midori Araki, Narukiyo, Phoenix, Rachel Chandler, Selgas Cano, Takashi Homma, Walter Pfeiffer.

Issue 6
Autumn/Winter 2010-11
Featuring: 6a Architects, Anders Edström, Carl Johan De Geer, Enric Ruiz Geli, Felisa Pinto, Frank Bruggeman, Gosha Rubchinskiy, Bernd Fraunholz, Leon Ransmeier, Leopoldo Pomés, Tiphaine De Lussy, Paz de la Huerta, Ramdane & Victorie Touhami, Tomi Ungerer.

Issue 7
Spring/Summer 2011
Featuring: Adan Jodorowsky Aldo & Marirosa Ballo, Alice Waters, Bruce Benderson, Chiara Merino and Claire Frisbie, Gloria & Anaïs, Jim Haynes, Juana Molina, Kenny Scharf, Liselotte Watkins, Mariuccia Casadio, Masha Orlov, Nestor Piriz, Ola Rindal, Vuokko Eskolin-Nurmesniemi, Zoe Bedeaux.

Issue 8
Autumn/Winter 2011-12
Featuring: Athena Currey, Beda Achermann, Ben Rivers, Brian Janusiak and Elizabeth Beer, Faye Toogood, Jan Demuynck, Jan Liégeois, Javier Mariscal, Makoto Orui, Marcelo Krasilcic, Nathalie Du Pasquier, Phillipe Parreno, Pilar Benitez Vibart, Valentine Fillol-Cordier.

Issue 9
Spring/Summer 2012
Featuring: Annabelle Dexter-Jones, Chris Johanson & Jo Jackson, Conor Donlon, Duncan Fallowell, Francesc Pla, Gonzalo Milà, Iñaki Baquero, India Salvor Menuez, Jeff Rian, José León Cerrillo, Nanos Valaoritis, Nic & Jackie Harrison, Nicolas Congé & Camille Berthomier, Reg Mombassa, Tierney Gearon, Tomás Nervi, Yrjö Kukkapuro.

Issue 10
Autumn/Winter 2012-13
Featuring: Andy Rementer & Margherita Urbani, Artus De Lavilleón, Aurora Altisent, Christophe Lemaire & Sarah-Linh Tran, David Toro & Solomon Chase, Devonté Hynes, Eduardo Longo, Edward Colver, Esther Mahlangu, Jim Walrod, Juan Stoppani, Ken Garland, Lisa Larson, Rachel Korine, Tauba Auerbach, Till Sperrle, Yorgos Lanthimos.

Covers

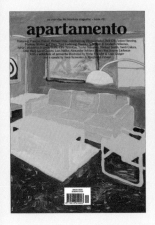

Issue 11
Spring/Summer 2013
Featuring: Andy Rementer
& Margherita Urbani, Anton
Henning, Apichatpong
Weerasethakul, Bob Gill,
Dike Blair, Elfie Semotan,
François Halard, JR &
Nelleke, Maurice Scheltens
& Liesbeth, Abbenes,
Michael Smith, Michael Stipe,
Ricardo Bofill, Santi Caleca,
Tenko Nakajima.

Issue 12
Autumn/Winter 2013-14
Featuring: Andy Rementer
& Margherita Urban,
Atsuki Kikuchi, Aurélien
Arbet & Jérémie Egry,
Christoph Ruckhäberle,
Chung Eun Mo, Genesis
P-Orridge, Ken Done, Moisés
Puente, Omar Souleyman,
Rose McGowan, Sara Sachs
& Frederik Jacobi, Scott
Ewalt, Scott Sternberg,
Smiljan Radic, Trix & Robert
Haussmann.

Issue 13
Spring/Summer 2014
Featuring: Alexander Girard,
Adel Husni Bey & Mirella,
Clemencigh, Anissa Helou,
Arturo Rhodes, Bernhard
Willhelm, Fabiola Alondra,
Jack Pierson, Jean-Charles
de Castelbajac, Joel Chen,
Lluís Clotet, Luciano Consigli,
Oscar Tusquets Blanca,
Peter Shire, Rafael Horzon,
Wes Anderson.

Issue 14
Autumn/Winter 2014-15
Featuring: Birgitta
Homburger & Florian Lambl,
Christiaan Houtenbos
Elena Quarestani, Heather
Boo & Claudia Schwalb,
Jeremiah Goodman,
Kenneth Perdigón, Koudlam,
Lora Lamm, Michael
Lindsay-Hogg, Neoptolemos
Michaelides, Oiva Toikka,
Peter Halley, Raymond
Pettibon, Terry Ellis.

Issue 15
Spring/Summer 2015
Featuring: Armin
Heinemann (Paula's Ibiza),
César Manrique, Donald
Cumming & Georgia Ford,
Gaspar Noé, Gene Krell,
Guy Rombouts, Linus Bill,
Marguerite Stephens,
Marvin & Ruth Sackner,
Matthew Stone, Ryan
McGinley, Shirana Shahbazi,
Todd Oldham, Vince Aletti.

Issue 16
Autumn/Winter 2015-16
Featuring: AA Bronson,
Arielle Holmes, David
Douglas Duncan, Denise
Scott Brown, Donald
Judd, Fernando Higueras,
Flavin & Rainer Judd, Gary
Panter, Guillermo Santomà,
Matt Connors, Pablo Picasso,
Philolaos, Xavier Corberó.

Issue 17
Spring/Summer 2016
Featuring: Abdul Mati
Klarwein, Danny Taylor,
Gage of the Boone, Jason
Schwartzman & Brady
Cunningham, Javier Perés,
Johann & Lena König,
Kathy Ryan, Klaus Biesenbach,
Liam Gillick, Martha Stewart,
Petra Collins, Raphaël Zarka,
Raúl de Nieves, The Spectrum,
Victoire de Castellane
& Thomas Lenthal.

Issue 18
Autumn/Winter 2016-17
Featuring: Andrea Zittel,
Bendetta Tagliabue,
Chloe Wise, Duncan Hannah,
Fernando Arrabal, JB Blunk,
Jeanne Greenberg Rohatyn,
Jessica Koslow, Kembra
Pfahler, Luis Venegas,
Margaret Howell, Molly
Goddard, Sébastien Meyer
& Arnaud Vaillant.

Issue 19
Spring/Summer 2017
Featuring: Alessandro
Mendini, Antoni Miralda,
Barbara Nessim, Bernard
Rudofsky's, Cristopher
Nying, Flawless Sabrina,
Ford Wheeler, Kim Hastreiter,
Leonard Koren, Naoki
Takizawa, Penny Martin,
Richard Hell, Robby Müller's
Polaroids.

Issue 20
Autumn/Winter 2017-18
Featuring: Andy Rementer
& Margherita Urbani,
Alec Soth, Gay Talese,
Jerry Schatzberg, Joseph
Holtzman, Julien Dossena,
Kyoichi Tsuzuki, Lawrence
Weiner, Margot & Fergus
Henderson, Maria Pratts,
Maureen Paley, Na Kim,
Office KGDVS.

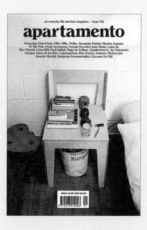

Featured in the magazine

AA Bronson*
Abdul Mati Klarwein*
Adan Jodorowsky*
Adel Husni Bey & Mirella
 Clemencigh*
Aldo & Marirosa Ballo
Alec Soth*
Aleishall, Alexis, Kori,
 & Marshall Girard*
Alessandro Mendini*
Alex Wiederin*
Alexandrea Singh
Alice Waters
Anders Ulla, Nils, Mai
 & Yoshiko Edström*
Andrea Zittel*
Anissa Helou
Annabelle Dexter-Jones
Anton Henning
Antoni Miralda
Apichatpong
 Weerasethakul*
Arielle Holmes*
Armin Heinemann*
Arturo Rhodes
Athena Currey
Atsuki Kikuchi
Audrey Fondecave-Tsujimura*
Aurélien Arbet
 & Jérémie Egry
Aurora Altisent
Aya Yamamoto
Barbara Nessim
Beda Achermann*
Ben Rivers
Benedetta Tagliabue
Benjamin Sommerhalder
Bernard Rudofsky
Bernhard Willhelm*
Bernd Fraunholz*
Bertjan Pot
Birgitta Homburger
 & Florian Lambl
Bob Gill
Brian Janusiak
 & Elizabeth Beer
Bruce Benderson
Carl Johan De Geer*
Carlotta Manaigo
César Manrique*
Charles Bessard
 & Nanne de Ru
Chloë Sevigny*
Chloe Wise
Chris Johanson & Jo Jackson
Christiaan Houtenbos*
Christoph Ruckhäberle
Christophe Lemaire
 & Sarah-Linh Tran*
Christopher Bollen*
Chung Eun Mo
Conor Donlon*
Cosima Gadient*
Craig Eberhardt
 & Julian Dorcelien*
Cristopher Nying
Cyril Duval*
Daniel Riera
Dante Bini
David Armstrong*
David Piper*
David Toro & Solomon Chase*
Denise Scott Brown*
Devonté Hynes*
Dike Blair*

Dominique Nabokov*
Donald Cumming
 & Georgia Ford
Donald Judd
Duncan Fallowell
Duncan Hannah*
Eduardo Longo*
Edward Colver*
Elein Fleiss*
Elena Quarestani*
Elfie Semotan*
Enzo Mari
Erol Alkan*
Esther Mahlangu*
Ezra Koenig*
Fabiola Alondra
Faye Toogood*
Felisa Pinto
Felix Friedmann*
Fernando Arrabal*
Fernando Higueras*
Flawless Sabrina*
Ford Wheeler*
Francesc Pla
François Halard*
Frank Bruggeman
Gage of the Boone, Danny
 Taylor & Raúl de Nieves*
Gary Panter
Gaspar Noé
Gay Talese
Gene Krell*
Genesis P-Orridge*
Maria Vittoria & Giorgio
 Backhaus*
Gloria Pinette
 & Anaïs Melero
Gonzalo Milà
Gosha Rubchinskiy*
Grillo Demo*
Guillermo Santomà
Gustavo Di Mario
Guy Rombouts
Heather Boo
 & Claudia Schwalb
Helen Maurer & Ted Barnes
Hugo de la Rosa
Imaad Wasif
India Salvor Menuez
Jack Pierson*
Jan Demuynck
Jan Lindenberg
Jason Schwartzman
 & Brady Cunningham*
Javier Mariscal
Javier Perés
JB Blunk
JD Samson
Jean Touitou
Jean-Charles de Castelbajac*
Jean-Philippe Delhomme*
Jeanne Greenberg Rohatyn
Jeff Rian
Jens Wicksen*
Jeremiah Goodman*
Jerry Schatzberg
Jessica Koslow
Jim Haynes*
Jim Walrod*
Joel Chen*
Johann & Lena König*
José León Cerrillo*
José Selgas
Joseph Holtzman*
Juan Stoppani

Juan Tessi
Juana Molina
Julian Gatto
Julien Dossena
Justin Bond*
Kathy Ryan
Kembra Pfahler*
Ken Done
Ken Garland
Kenneth Perdigón
Kenny Scharf*
Kersten Geers
 & David Van Severen
Kim Hastreiter*
Klaus Biesenbach*
Koudlam
Kyoichi Tsuzuki*
Lawrence Weiner*
Leon Ransmeier*
Leonard Koren*
Leopoldo Pomés
Liam Gillick*
Linus Bill*
Lisa Larson
Liselotte Watkins
Lora Lamm*
Lovefoxxx*
Lucía Cano
Luis Venegas
Luiza Sá
Luna Paiva & Leandro Erlich*
Madoka & Ola Rindal*
Makoto Orui*
Marc Frohn
 & Mario Rojas Toledo
Marcelo Krasilcic*
Margaret Howell*
Margot & Fergus Henderson*
Marguerite Stephens*
Maria Pratts*
Mark Sladen & Garrick Jones
Markus Miessen
Martha Stewart
Martino Gamper
Marvin & Ruth Sackner*
Masha Orlov
Mathias Sterner
Matt Connors
Matthew Stone*
Maureen Paley*
Maurice Scheltens
 & Liesbeth Abbenes*
Max Lamb*
Michael Lindsay-Hogg
Michael Smith
Michael Stipe*
Midori Araki
Mike Mills*
Molly Goddard*
Mylinh Trieu Nguyen*
Mystery Jets*
Na Kim*
Nanos Valaoritis*
Naoki Takizawa
Narukiyo Yoshida*
Nathalie Du Pasquier*
Nelleke McCowan
 & JR Reynolds
Neoptolemos Michaelides*
Nestor Piriz
Nic & Jackie Harrison
Nicolas Congé
 & Camille Berthomier*
Oiva Toikka*
Omar Souleyman*

Oscar Tusquets Blanca*
Pablo Picasso
Paul Schiek
Paulo César Pereio
Paz de la Huerta*
Penny Martin
Peter Halley*
Peter Shire*
Petra Collins*
Philip Crangi
Phillippe Parreno
Philolaos*
Phoenix
Pilar Benítez Vibart
Rachel Chandler
Rachel Korine*
Rafael Horzon*
Rainer & Flavin Judd*
Ramdane Touhami
 & Victorie de Taillac-Touhami
Ramon Perez*
Raphaël Zarka
Raymond Pettibon
Reg Mombassa
Ricardo Bofill*
Richard Hell*
Richard & Cosmo Wise
RJ Shaughnessy
Robby Müller
Rose McGowan*
Rudolf Steiner
Ryan McGinley*
Santi Caleca
Sara Sachs
 & Frederik Jacobi*
Scott Ewalt
Scott Sternberg
Sébastien Meyer
 & Arnaud Vaillant
Shauna Toohey
 & Misha Hollenbach
Shirana Shahbazi*
Skye Parrott
Smiljan Radic
Sonic Youth
Sonya Park*
Stella Sabin
Stephanie Macdonald
 & Tom Emerson
Takashi Homma
Tatiana Bilbao
Tauba Auerbach*
Tenko Nakajima*
Terence Koh*
Terry Ellis*
Tierney Gearon*
Till Sperrle
Tiphaine De Lussy*
Todd Oldham*
Tomás Nervi*
Tomi Ungerer*
Trix & Robert Haussmann*
Valentine Fillol-Cordier*
Victoire de Castellane
 & Thomas Lenthal*
Vince Aletti*
Vuokko Eskolin-Nurmesniemi
Walter Pfeiffer*
Wes Anderson
Xavier Corberó*
Yorgo Tloupas*
Yorgos Lanthimos*
Yrjö Kukkapuro*
Zoe Bedeaux*

Contributors

We would like to express our sincere thanks to our dear contributors for putting up with us over all these years. We would quite literally be nowhere without your generosity and dedication.

Contributors
Åbäke
Achim Hatzius
Ada Bligaard Søby
Adam Saletti
Adam Yarinsky
Adan Jodorowsky
Adrià Cañameras
Adrià Julià
Adrian Gaut
Adrian Walter
Adrianna Glaviano
Agnes Chemetov
Ai Weiwei
Albert Moya
Alberto Pellegrinet
Alejandra Smits
Alessandro Gori
Alessandro Mendini
Alex Gartenfeld
Alex Tieghi-Walker
Alexander Elzesser
Alexander Girard
Alexander Heminway
Alexander Kori Girard
Alexander Schärer
Alexander von Vegesack
Alexandre Bettler
Alexandre Fehr
Alia Farid Abdal
Alice Cavanagh
Alice Fiorilli
Alisée Matta
Amanda Maxwell
Amelia Stein
Ana Armendariz
Ana Cuba
Ana Dominguez
Ana Kraš
Ana Margarida Figueiredo Braga
Anders Edström
Andrea Bocco Guarneri
Andrea Lissoni
Andrea Zittel
Andrew Kuo
Andrew Zuckerman
Andy Beach
Andy Rementer
Angelo Pennetta
Anja Aronowsky Cronberg
Anna Clerici
Anna von Löw
Anne Waak
Annette Merrild
Anri Sala
Antonio Montouto
Ari Marcopoulos
Arielle Holmes
Artus de Lavilléon
Atsuki Kikuchi
Audrey Fondecave-Tsujimura
Aya Sekine
Aya Yamamoto
Ben Rivers
Benjamin Fredrickson
Benjamin Pardo

Benjamin Sommerhalder
Benoît Wolfrom
Bert Krus
Bertjan Pot
Betta Marzio
Bless
Brett Lloyd
Cameron Allan McKean
Carl Johan De Geer
Carlie Armstrong
Carlos Chavarría
Carlota Guerrero
Carlota Santamaria
Carlotta Manaigo
Carol Montpart
Carol Reid-Gaillard
Catherine Krudy
Charlie Koolhaas
Chiara Merino
Chloé More
Chloë Sevigny
Christian Mazzalai
Christopher Bollen
Claire Frisbie
Clarke Tolton
Claudette Didul
Claudia Roden
Clemency Jones
Clemens Kois
Coke Bartrina
Coryander Friend
Cosimo Bizzarri
Courtney Utt
Cris Merino
Damien Florébert Cuypers
Daniel Morgenthaler
Daniel Riera
Daniel Terna
Daniel Trese
Danielle Pender
Dante Bini
David Armstrong
David Belisle
David Douglas Duncan
David John
David Piper
David Torcasso
David Van Severen
Dean Kissick
Deidi von Schaewen
Delfino Sisto Legnani
Devendra Banhart
Deyan Sudjic
Dominic Broadhurst
Dominique Nabokov
Douglas Lance Gibson
Dru Donovan
Eduardo Longo
Edwin Heathcote
Ekhi Lopetegi
Elein Fleiss
Elena Quarestani
Elisabeth Moch
Elliot Beaumont
Elo Vázquez
Elsa Beach
Elsa Fischer
Emanuele Fontanesi
Emily King
Emily Robertson
Enric Ruiz-Geli
Enrique Giner de los Ríos
Erik Wåhlström
Eva Hagberg
Evangelia Koutsovoulou

Ezra Koenig
FAR
Faye Toogood
Federica Sala
Felisa Pinto
Felix Burrichter
Felix Friedmann
Fernando Amat
Fernando Lloveras
Flavin Judd
Fouad Abousaada
Francesc Pla
Francesc Pons
Francesco Spampinato
Francesco Zanot
François Halard
Frank Bruggeman
Franziska Sinn
Frederike Helwig
Gemma Holt
Geoff McFetridge
George Sowden
Georgie Hopton
Giacomo De Poli
Gian Gisiger
Gianluigi Ricuperati
Giorgiana Ravizza
Giorgio Di Salvo
Giovanna Silva
Gisela Filc
Gonzalo Milà
Gosha Rubchinskiy
Grillo Demo
Guillermo Santomà
Gunnar Knechtel
Hanayo
Hanna Nilsson
Hasisi Park
Helena Strängberg Velardi
Hélène Binet
Henry Roy
Hillary Navin
Hiroshi Eguchi
Hisae Mizutani
Hisashi Okawa
Hugo de la Rosa
Hugo Macdonald
Ida Kukkapuro
Ida Nordén
Imaad Wasif
Iñaki Baquero
India Salvor Menuez
Isa Merino
Isabel Mallet
Ivan Carvalho
Iwan Baan
Jaap Scheeren
Jack Self
Jacob Åström
Jacquelyn Thompson
Jae Seok Kim
James Jarvis
James Ross-Edwards
Jan Bitter
Jan Demuynck
Jan Liégeois
Jason Frank Rothenberg
Jason Nocito
Jean Abou
Jean-Philippe Delhomme
Jeff Rian
Jem Goulding
Jenna Sutela
Jeremy Liebman
Jessica Piersanti

Jim Stoten
Joan Morey
Joana Avillez
Jocko Weyland
Jody Rogac
Joe Magliaro
Jolanthe Kugler
Jonathan Heaf
Jonathan Olivares
Jonathan Openshaw
Jordi Ferreiro
Jordi Labanda
Jordi Tió
Jordy van den Nieuwendijk
Jorge de Cascante
Jorge M Fontana
Jose Arnaud
José Hevia
José Juan Ramírez
José Manuel Ábalos
Josefin Hellström Olsson
Josep Fonti
Josh Lieberman
Juan Ignacio Moralejo
Juan Moralejo
Juergen Teller
Julian Gatto
Julie Cirelli
Justin McGuirk
JW Anderson
Kaarle Hurtig
Karin Weiborg
Karley Sciortino
Kasane Nogawatakas
Kasia Bobula
Kat Herriman
Katarina Šoškic
Katherine Clary
Kathy Ryan
Ken Miller
Kenneth Perdigón
Kersten Geers
Kiko Buxo
KK Barrett
Klas Ernflo
Klas Fahlén
Koen Sels
Kris Latocha
Kristin Loschert
Kuba Ryniewicz
Lars Laemmerzahl
Lars Müller
Laura Regensdorf
Laurent Brancowitz
Lawrence Weiner
Leen Hilde Haesen
Leila McAlister
Lele Saveri
Lena C Emery
Leon Ransmeier
Leslie Williamson
Li Edelkoort
Lilian Martinez
Linlee Allen
Linus Bill
Lluís Clotet
Lola Botia
Louise Melchior
Lovefoxxx
Lovis Caputo
Luis Cerveró
Luiza Sá
Lukas Wassmann
Madeline Gannon
Marcelo Krasilcic

Contributors

Margherita Urbani
María Corte
Maria Cristina Didero
Maria Gerhardt
Mariah Nielson
Marie Honda
Marisa Brickman
Mariuccia Casadio
Mark Borthwick
Mark Mahaney
Mark Wasiuta
Markus Miessen
Marlene Marino
Marta Riezu
Martino Gamper
Masahiro Sanbe
Masamichi Udagawa
Mateo Kries
Mathias Sterner
Matt Connors
Matt Leines
Matt Paweski
Matthew Freemantle
Max Lamb
Maya Handley
Michael Anastassiades
Michael Sieber
Michael Stipe
Michy Marxuach
Mieke Verbijlen
Miguel Figueroa
Mike Abelson
Mike Meiré
Mike Mills
Milano Chow
Miranda July
Mirella Clemencigh
Mirko Borsche
Misha Hollenbach
Misha Janette
Mo Veld
Moisés Puente
Monica Canilao
Mylinh Trieu Nguyen
Nan Goldin
Nancy Waters
Nathalie Du Pasquier
Neil Gavin
Nestor Piriz
Nicholas Lander
Nick Currie
Nico Krijno
Nicola Enrico Stäubli
Nicolas Congé
Nicolas Trembley
Nicole Bachmann
Nolaster
Nuria Olivella
Ola Rindal
Olaf Breuning
Olimpia Zagnoli
Oscar Grønner
Oscar Peña
Oscar Tusquets Blanca
Osma Harvilahti
Pablo Castro
Paloma Lanna
Patricia Urquiola
Patrick Parrish
Patrizia Moroso
Pau Guinart
Paul Schiek
Paula Yacomuzzi
Pavel Milyakov
Pepe Carballido

Peter Halley
Peter Odevall
Petra Collins
Philippe Parreno
Piero Gandini
Pieter Van Eenoge
Pilar Viladas
Piotr Niepsuj
Porzia Bergamasco
Quentin de Briey
Rafael de Cardenas
Ramak Fazel
Ramdane Touhami
Raphaël Zarka
Rene Vaile
Retts Wood
Ricardo Fumanal
Richard Jensen
Richard Kern
Richard McConkey
RJ Shaughnessy
Robby Müller
Roberta Ridolfi
Roz Jana
Rui Tenreiro
Rujana Rebernjak
Ryan Conder
Ryan Lowry
Ryan Willms
Sabine Magnet
Sabrina Tarasoff
Sam Grawe
Sandy Kim
Scott A Sant'Angelo
Sean Kinnerly
Sean Michael Beolchini
Selgas Cano
Serkan Taycan
Shelby Duncan
Silvia Orlandi
Silvia Robertazzi
Simon Castets
Skye Parrott
Smiljan Radic
Sofia Østerhus
Soraya Rosales
Susan Sellers
Tag Christof
Takashi Homma
Tankboys
Taro Hirano
Tatiana Bilbao
Tauba Auerbach
Tenko Nakajima
Terry Richardson
Thea Slotover
Thomas Dozol
Thomas Jeppe
Tierney Gearon
Till Sperrle
Tim Barber
Tim Elkaïm
Tim Lahan
Tim Small
Tina Barney
Todd Oldham
Tomás Nervi
Tony Cederteg
Ulrich Lamsfuss
Ute Woltron
Valentina Ciuffi
Vassilis Karidis
Victoire Touhami
Victoria Camblin
Victoria Hely-Hutchinson

Viktor Hachmang
Vince Aletti
Vincent Dilio
Wai Lin Tse
Walter Pfeiffer
Wes Del Val
Witold Rybczynski
Wolfgang Tillmans
Xavier Marset
Yasmine Dubois-Ziai
Ye Rin Mok
Yoko Amakawa
Yorgo Tloupas
Yukari Miya

Special Thanks

Aitor Fuentes Mendizabal,
Albert Folch, Aitor Murillo,
Alba Donis, Ana Dominguez,
Andreas Pritchard, Andreu
Llos, Antonio Sosa,
Ariel Schulman, Belinda
Wicksteed, Benjamin
Sommerhalder, Blanca
Alegre, Bruce Benderson,
CA Grafica, Cristina
Carulla, David Oliver, David
Peñuela, David Zwirner,
Davies Costacurta, Débora
Antscherl, Elsa Ahlbom,
Eric Hesselbo, Esther
Morell, Felix Burrichter,
Fiona Wylie, Fred Dechnik,
Giorgiana Ravizza, Giovanni
Galilei, Helena Strängberg
Velardi, Henriette Kruse,
Igor Urdampilleta, Jackie
Willis, Jonathan Bennett,
Jordi Labanda Julia Worley,
Katherine Clary, Kim
Hastreiter, Laila Gohar,
Leah Singer, Leen Hilde
Haesen, Laura Grabalosa,
Luciano Cirelli Maddalena
Vatti, Lluís Masdevall, María
Sosa Betancor, Massimo
Torrigiani, Michela Pelizzari,
Miles Fischler, Miriam
Gerace, Paul Geddis, Paul
Kopkau, Pablo Bofill, Pilar
Benitez Vibart, Richard
Figueroa, Stefanie Doerper,
Sean Michael Beolchini,
Susan Whitehead, Teddy
Iborra Wicksteed, Esperanza
Valero, Titi Maza, Varda
Sokolowicz, Víctor Abellan
and Victor Poll

This book is dedicated to our
families; without their love
and support *Apartamento*
wouldn't even exist.

Apartamento Magazine

Founders
Nacho Alegre
Omar Sosa
Marco Velardi

Managing Editor
Robbie Whitehead

Content Editor
Madeleine Willis

Distribution Manager
Júlia Poll Morell

Editorial Assistant
Laura Frade

Contributing Editors
Arquitectura-G
Alix Browne
Haydée Touitou
Jim Walrod
Leah Singer
Michael Bullock

App Developer
The Exposed

Edited by Omar Sosa, Nacho Alegre, and Marco Velardi

Graphic Design: Apartamento Studios
Content Editor: Madeleine Willis
Project Manager: Robbie Whitehead
Assistant: Laura Frade

Abrams Editor: Holly Dolce
Production Manager: Katie Gaffney
Abrams Managing Editor: Mary O'Mara

Library of Congress Control Number: 2017949750

ISBN: 978-1-4197-2892-1
eISBN: 978-1-68335-226-6

Printed and bound in China
10 9 8 7 6 5 4

www.apartamentomagazine.com

ABRAMS
The Art of Books

195 Broadway
New York, NY 10007
abramsbooks.com

A Fresh Start, a comic by Andy Rementer & Margherita Urbani. 2014.

'I sleep about four hours a night, so I get up early. The first thing I do is work out what sport I'm going to play that day.'
Devonté Hynes, New York City. Interview by Karley Sciortino. Photography by Sandy Kim. 2012.

'I realise how important it is to be a fan of everyone you're working with and to do things that are in your heart. Unfortunately that makes it so I don't know anything about anything I'm not interested in, and I can't do anything that I'm not passionate about.'
Todd Oldham, New York City. Interview by Alexander Kori Girard. Photography by Jason Frank Rothenberg. 2015.

'Richard moved into the house last October.'
Richard & Cosmo Wise, London. Text and photography by Aya Sekine. 2010.

'I don't want to be so dogmatic about how I live and what I live with. There is too much control at the extremities.'
Leonard Koren, Point Reyes. Interview by Mariah Nielson. Photography by Carlos Chavarría. 2017.

'I wrote two albums in this house, I was seated on my red couch. I need the red to create. It's the colour of my blood, I feel alive when I touch it.'
Adan Jodorowsky, Paris. Text by Adan Jodorowsky. Photography by Shelby Duncan. 2011.

'She had her bedroom set custom made at Twentieth in LA, matching the colour to a bottle of nail polish.'
Rose McGowan, Los Angeles. Text and photography by Marlene Marino. 2013.

Zoe Bedeaux, London. Interview by Anja Aronowsky Cronberg. Photography by Juergen Teller. 2011.

'We arrived at the house in the early evening not knowing that we would be trapped there for the next two days.
Winter broke through all of a sudden with such a power, so much snow, so few sights.'
Bernd Fraunholz, Germany. Text and photography by Kristin Loschert. 2010.

Opposite: 'We do drink a lot of tea, cook some nice stuff, and hang out half-naked.'
Camille Berthomier & Nicolas Congé (Jehnny Beth & Johnny Hostile), London. Text by Nicolas Congé. Photography by Jem Goulding. 2012.

'I always imagined that doctors, lawyers, or notaries lived there, and that they had neatly organised libraries with leather-bound books, antique furniture, silver cutlery, neo-romantic landscape paintings on the walls.'
Guy Rombouts, Antwerp. Text by Koen Sels. Photography by Mieke Verbijlen. 2015.

'Initially, putting blinds up in the bathroom wasn't as important as the electricity, so it simply never happened; now they like to joke they're performing a service for the neighbours.'
The zombie porn factory, London. Text by David Piper. Photography by Marco Velardi. 2009.

'I would typically meet someone in a bar and ask, "What kind of place are you living in?" Then I might ask if I could photograph their room.
Once I was inside, I'd ask, "Do you have friends around here I can visit, too?" Sometimes they'd say, "Yeah, I know the person who lives next door—let's go".
But often no one would answer the buzzer, so they might say, "I know where the key is, let's go inside, I'll tell them later".'
Kyoichi Tsuzuki, 2017. Interview by Cameron Allan McKean. Photography by Kyoichi Tsuzuki, from *Tokyo Style*, 1993.

'I can't say I like it because when I'm searching for something, especially a paper or an article, I lose time. I'm not very systematic.'
Nanos Valaoritis, Athens. Interview by Evangelia Koutsovoulou. Photography by Vassilis Karidis. 2012.

Ramon Perez, Paris. Photography by Nacho Alegre. 2008.

'The way a book appears completely determines whether I'm interested in it or not. There are times when I might like the contents but I can't bear the graphic design, so I really can't have it here.'
Vince Aletti, New York City. Interview by Paul Schiek. Photography by Jason Nocito. 2015.

'One option is that you have to make something expensive so then people have to question themselves, to make a decision: if they will buy it in the first place, and then if they want to keep it. And the other way is trying to make it yourself.' Max Lamb, London. Text by Paula Yacomuzzi. Photography by Marco Velardi. 2008.

'I think if you do something very seriously and sincerely, then there's always something that remains even if it's not fashionable anymore. It's only things that are done without the heart that don't last.' Nathalie Du Pasquier, Milan. Interview by Helena Nilsson Strängberg. Photography by Alice Fiorilli. 2011.

'Gomringer's idea was that in original concrete poetry, you should only use nouns. You should not use verbs because the viewer should try to connect the dots to find the meaning.'
Ruth & Marvin Sackner, Miami. Interview by Leah Singer. Photography by Ryan Lowry, 2015.

Ruth & Marvin Sackner, Miami. Interview by Leah Singer. Photography by Ryan Lowry. 2015.

Deep Fried Squirrel

One squirrel per person

Ingredients

Squirrel: cut into two shoulders, saddle and two hind legs

Pig's trotters, one to every four squirrel

Whole heads of garlic, one to every four squirrel

A glass of Vieille Prune

Light chicken stock

Seasoned flour

Eggs whisked with a fork into egg wash

Very fine breadcrumbs. The fineness of the crumb is vital, so you end up with just a whisper of batter between you and the squirrel.

Vegetable oil for frying

Place trotters, garlic and stock (enough to cover your jointed squirrel) in a pot. Bring to a boil then reduce to a simmer for 3 hours, allowing the trotters to emit their goodness.

Take off the heat, add glass of Vieille Prune and the squirrel pieces. Cover pot and put in a very gentle oven for 1 1/2 to 2 hours, checking with a knife so that the flesh feels. When ready, remove the trotters and squirrel from the liquor, as it will make a stunning squirrel broth.

Once squirrel is cold, lightly flour, egg and cover with breadcrumbs.

'If someone has their first flat, they go to buy furniture, and the first thing they buy today is a sofa so they can watch TV,
rather than a table to eat at, which is both sad and weird for me.'
Margot & Fergus Henderson, London. Interview by Hugo Macdonald. Photography by Angelo Pennetta. 2017.

'I suppose it's a modified Northern California woodsy, modernist structure, but it is actually pretty plain and anonymous.'
Leonard Koren, Point Reyes. Interview by Mariah Nielson. Photography by Carlos Chavarría. 2017.

'All I need is a bottle of champagne to hang a new painting.'
Trix & Robert Haussmann, Zurich. Interview by Daniel Morgenthaler. Photography by Lukas Wassmann. 2013.

'I've never regretted not building a box.'
Yrjö Kukkapuro, Helsinki. Interview by Ida Kukkapuro. Photography by Osma Harvilahti. 2012.

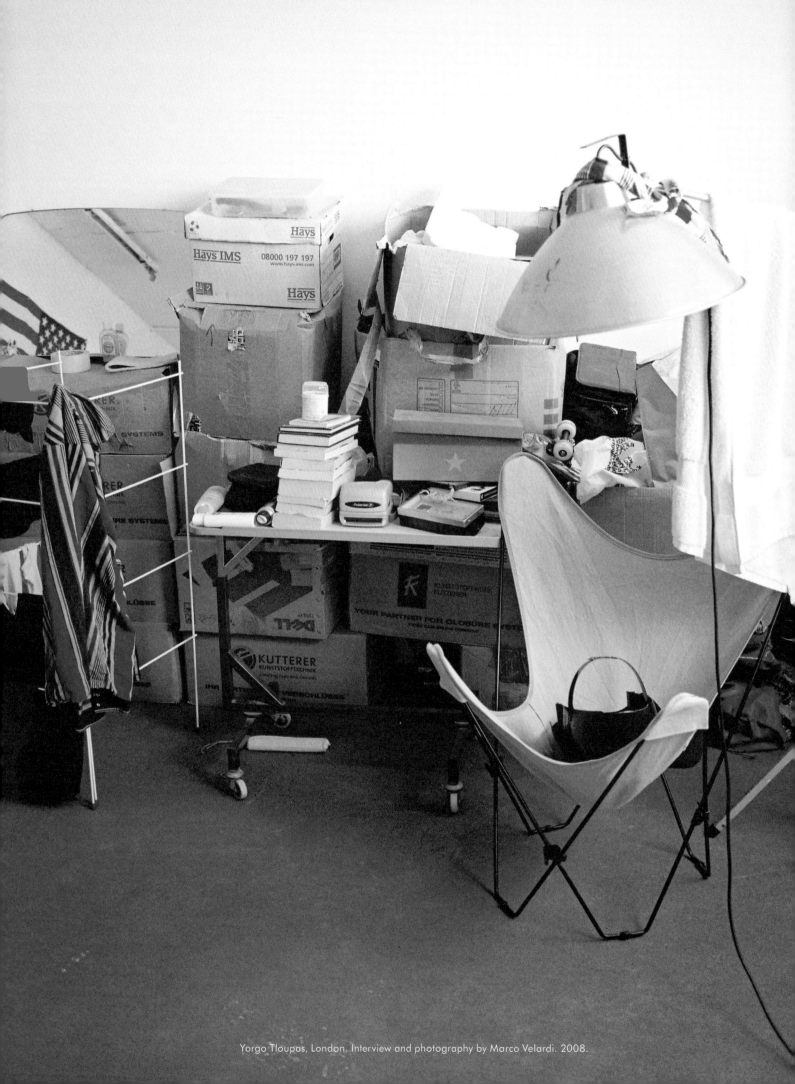

Yorgo Tloupas, London. Interview and photography by Marco Velardi. 2008.

'It's a studio house, where you work and live, not a villa beside the lake.'
Beda Achermann, Zurich. Interview by David Torcasso. Photography by Walter Pfeiffer. 2011.

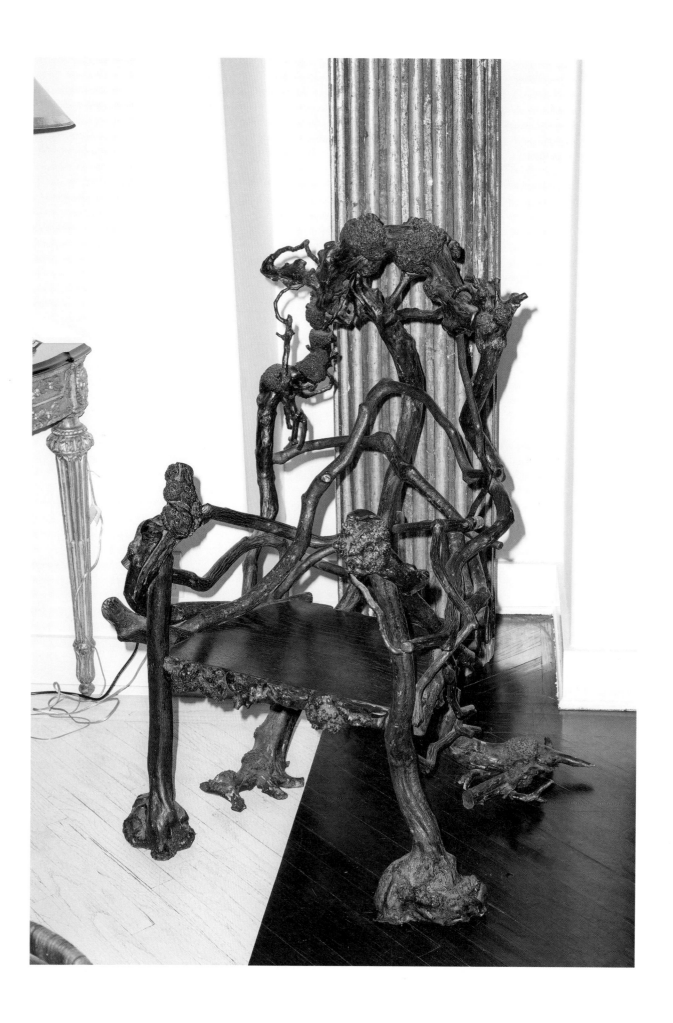

'I'm looking for the next wave. I don't like the idea of the next wave, but business-wise you need to be keen on all that.'
Joel Chen, Los Angeles. Interview by Jonathan Olivares. Photography by Jeremy Liebman. 2014.

'I think Don was interested in delivering certain things if we really requested them. I mean, we got desks.'
Rainer & Flavin Judd, Las Casas, Texas. Interview by Alix Browne. Photography by Ryan Lowry. 2015.

Beda Achermann, Zurich. Interview by David Torcasso. Photography by Walter Pfeiffer. 2011.

Opposite: 'I hope that for younger creative people, interacting with their peers, learning from them, and supporting them is still at the core of everything.'
Peter Halley, New York City. Interview by Jim Walrod. Photography by Jeremy Liebman. 2014.

'Eating at really fancy restaurants in other cities. Flying home. Making up. Finally saying it. Believing more. Rediscovering Joseph Cornell collages. Eating at that Cajun restaurant in Nevada City. Milkshakes. Oh yeah, I should exercise. Everyone who died gets to come back for lunch.'
Mike Mills, Los Angeles. Photography by Ye Rin Mok. 2008.

'In 1991 Scotland Yard raided my two homes ... They decided that I was a wrecker of civilisation and a satanist, of all things.'
Genesis P-Orridge, New York City. Interview by Devendra Banhart. Photography by Ana Kraš. 2013.

'Remember when you wanted a small office that was just a bed with a laptop station? We were thinking the sheets would be tucked in really tight. It wouldn't be like "get into bed", but more like "bed workspace".'
David Toro & Solomon Chase, New York City. Interview by Michael Bullock. Photography by Benjamin Fredrickson. 2012.

'I only listen to Björk.'
Omar Souleyman, Urfa. Interview by Alia Farid. Photography by Serkan Taycan. 2013.

Ulla, Nils, Mai, and Yoshiko Edström, Tokyo. Text and photography by Anders Edström. 2010.

'Years ago when I did *Broken Manual* I really wanted to buy a cave; I was fixated on this idea of a cave and I took it seriously and I began shopping for one ...
The big question from my family was, "Well, what are you going to do in the cave?" And I was like, "Uh, I'm going to sit in my cave and think about my childhood".'
Alec Soth, Minneapolis. Interview by Paul Schiek. Photography by Dru Donovan. 2017.

Tierney Gearon, Los Angeles. Interview by Alice Cavanagh. Photography by Tierney Gearon. 2012.

'Especially since this is an Ikea bed, you need to put a little message on it. It says,
"Bernhard, your mother is proud of you, Bernhard, your father is proud of you".'
Bernhard Willhelm, Los Angeles. Interview by Michael Bullock. Photography by Daniel Trese. 2014.

Opposite: George Condo, Paris, 1994. Text and painting by Grillo Demo. 2009.

'Add a badly maintained garden and you have an approximately 700m2 surface that you simply can't miss in a neighbourhood
so polished that people compete over having the best-cut grass.'
Jens Wicksen, Stockholm. Text and photography by Mathias Sterner. 2008.

'But, you know, furniture designers and product designers, there's not a lot of sex appeal and for a good reason.'
Leon Ransmeier, New York City. Interview by Michael Bullock. Photography by Nacho Alegre. 2010.

Opposite: 'Owning a house is the scariest thing to me—this thing that you buy is where you're supposed to be for the rest of your life.
And I'm not sure that that's something I want.'
Petra Collins, New York City. Interview by Jim Walrod. Photography by Tim Barber. 2016.

'We tend to work only with people sharing the same vibe, sometimes in their own different ways,
even if that means less money or less ambition, fuck it, people first.'
Camille Berthomier & Nicolas Congé (Jehnny Beth & Johnny Hostile), London. Text by Nicolas Congé. Photography by Jem Goulding. 2012.

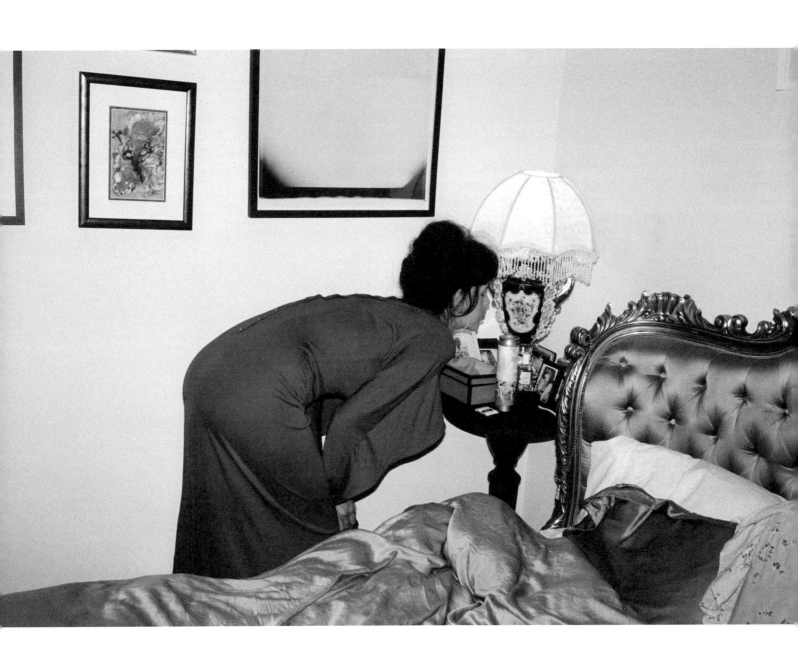

Paz de la Huerta, New York City. Photography by Marlene Marino. 2010.

'I didn't come following a dream. I think it's very important to understand that you do these things out of necessity and suffering. The idea of something better comes together with that. It's not that you are halfway comfortable and think of changing your life.' Armin Heinemann, Ibiza. Interview and photography by Nacho Alegre. 2015.

'What was interesting for me was that rock 'n roll had all these various means of communicating and one of them was the way you dressed.
And I thought about what I wanted the way I dressed to say.'
Richard Hell, New York City. Interview by Jim Walrod. Photography by Richard Kern. 2017.

Opposite: 'I do many things at home, like editing the music I play in my restaurant, repairing dishware. Also, when I'm home, my wife cooks for me!'
Narukiyo, Tokyo. Interview by Yoko Amakawa. Photography by Marco Velardi. 2010.

'I wanted to be diligent, for everything to be in order, each item in its proper place. I even had a place for shoes by the front door, but of course no one ever used it: I didn't have enough authority to make everyone roam the house barefoot, like in a Hindu temple.'
Elena Quarestani, Milan. Text by Elena Quarestani. Photography by Delfino Sisto Legnani. 2014.

Opposite: Linus Bill, Bienne. Text and photography by Linus Bill. 2008.

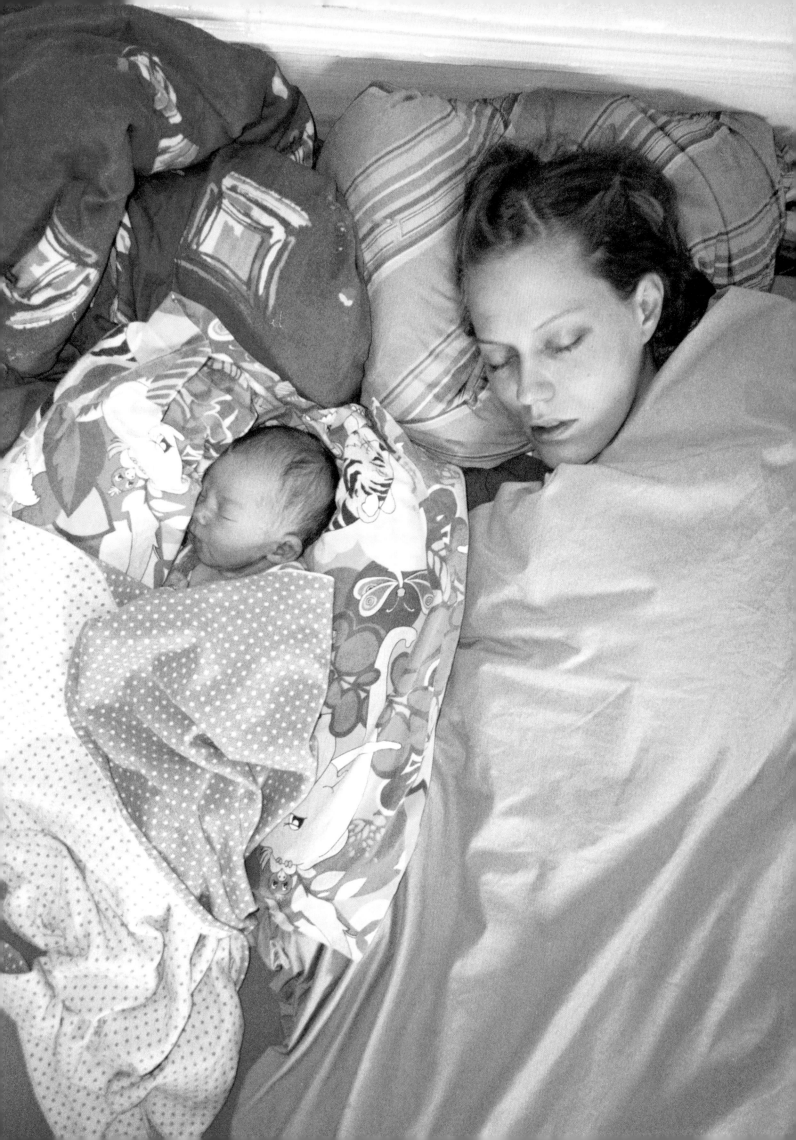

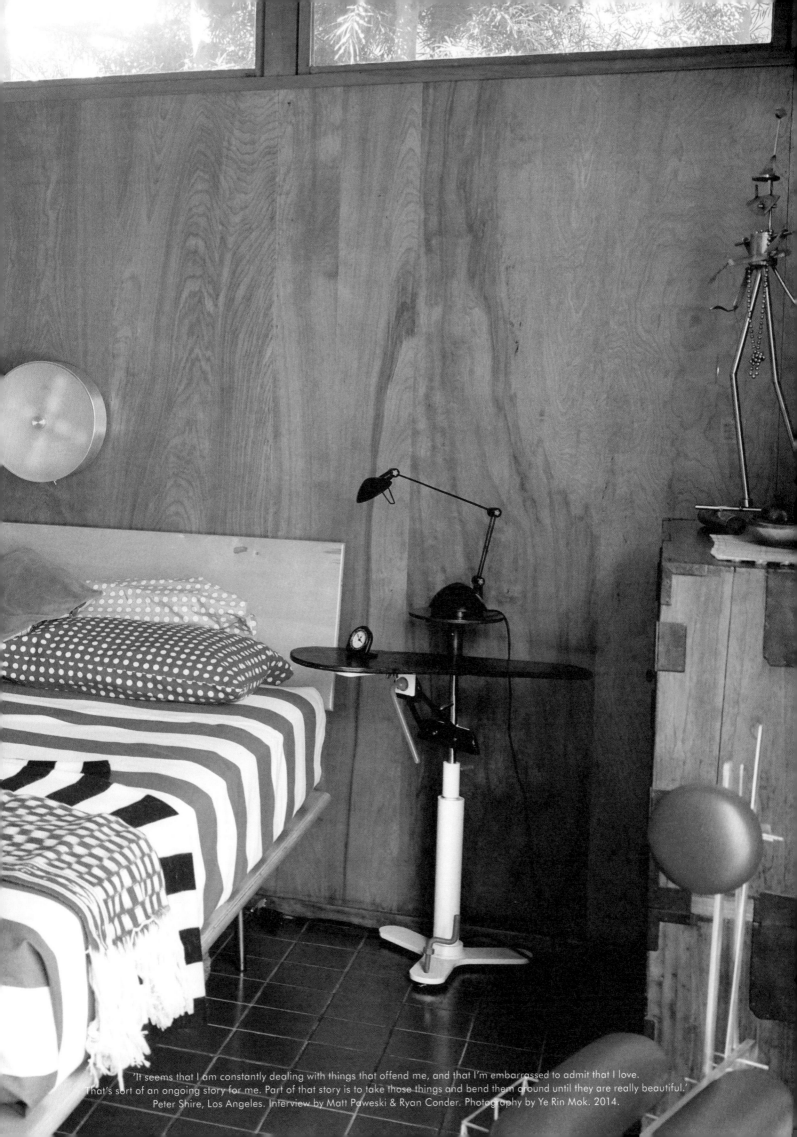

'It seems that I am constantly dealing with things that offend me, and that I'm embarrassed to admit that I love. That's sort of an ongoing story for me. Part of that story is to take those things and bend them around until they are really beautiful.' Peter Shire, Los Angeles. Interview by Matt Paweski & Ryan Conder. Photography by Ye Rin Mok. 2014.

Oiva Toikka, Helsinki. Interview by Ida Kukkapuro. Photography by Osma Harvilahti. 2014.

'When you enter a place, you pay attention to it through some tricks of irregularity. It's like with the proportions of a piece of furniture: if you make them a little bit wrong, instead of making them all right, you create a tension.'
Alessandro Mendini, Milan. Interview by Gianluigi Ricuperati. Photography by Piotr Niepsuj. 2017.

'Basquiat was a drug addict and I wasn't into that, but I knew one of his coke dealers. This dealer used to call me in the middle of the night saying, "I have one of Jean's painted doors that you can have, if you can get $1,000 to me in the next hour and bring it to Avenue B".' Kim Hastreiter, New York City. Interview by Michael Stipe. Photography by Tina Barney. 2017.

Opposite: 'I have totally given up on the idea of keeping up with things since I moved to New York, whether it's doing my laundry at responsible intervals, or seeing all the shows and performances I'd like to see. It's impossible. But that's what's so great about New York, too: there's too much.' Tauba Auerbach, New York City. Interview and photography by Luiza Sá. 2012.

'If I'm getting ready for a new show, I'll repaint the walls Tile Red, scrub all the windows,
and move all the objects from one side of the house to the other.'
Kembra Pfahler, New York City. Interview by Michael Bullock. Photography by Vincent Dilio. 2016.

'There was a type of home when I first came to New York City that felt like a "New York" space, and those apartments don't really exist anymore because of the gentrification of New York City. But the space we are in now is one of those remaining dream homes that I thought existed.'
Jim Walrod, New York City. Interview by Patrick Parrish. Photography by Jeremy Liebman. 2012.

'I'd like to have nothing on the walls. Liberated. Because then everything would be possible on the remaining white wall.'
Victoire de Castellane & Thomas Lenthal, Paris. Interview by Haydée Touitou. Photography by Frederike Helwig. 2016.

Opposite: 'I don't believe false modesty is a virtue. I created glam rock. I did it. It was very intentional.'
Gene Krell, Tokyo. Interview by Jim Walrod. Photography by Jeremy Liebman. 2015.

Peter Halley, New York City. Interview by Jim Walrod. Photography by Jeremy Liebman. 2014.

'We both seem to be interested in the stranger works of artists. Not the likeable ones, but the ones that show the true character of an artist.
The ones that are not really meant to be looked at, or to be sold, but where something just had to get out.'
Trix & Robert Haussmann, Zurich. Interview by Daniel Morgenthaler. Photography by Lukas Wassmann. 2013.

'I have a very clear mental image of eating on the floor while leaning against this wall in the kitchen with nothing in the apartment the first night.'
Tauba Auerbach, New York City. Interview and photography by Luiza Sá. 2012.

Oiva Toikka, Helsinki. Interview by Ida Kukkapuro. Photography by Osma Harvilahti. 2014.

'My garage's renovation took four years, but it's still unfinished, and not perfect for everyday life.'
Makoto Orui, Paris. Text by Makoto Orui. Photography by Ola Rindal. 2011.

'Catastrophes are beautiful, when one is not in the middle of them.'
Oiva Toikka, Helsinki. Interview by Ida Kukkapuro. Photography by Osma Harvilahti. 2014.

Opposite: Ruth & Marvin Sackner, Miami. Interview by Leah Singer. Photography by Ryan Lowry. 2015.

'At one time I had the feeling that as soon as someone became a widow, she suddenly started to paint. I wanted to avoid that.'
Lora Lamm, Zurich. Interview by Daniel Morgenthaler. Photography by Lukas Wassmann. 2014.

'Designing a space for someone is like giving a present. You can't wait to see how peoples' faces react to this space you have made.'
Faye Toogood, London. Interview by Marco Velardi. Photography by Roberta Ridolfi. 2011.

'Most of America was either urban or suburban, while New Mexico was this rough, funky, still kind of Wild West state where people were trading all kinds of handmade goods.'
Feature on Alexander Girard & the Girard family, Santa Fe. Interview by Marco Velardi. Photography by Nacho Alegre. 2014.

Opposite: Alex Wiederin, New York City. Interview by Katherine Clary. Photography by Nacho Alegre. 2010.

Dominique Nabokov, 2010. Interview by Anja Aronowsky Cronberg. Photography by Dominique Nabokov: Francesco Clemente's
living room, New York, 1997, from *New York Living Rooms*.

Opposite: 'Art historians like to keep artists alive by discussing their history in terms of the anthropological, the sociological, and the political.
But I always thought artists were kept alive by other artists.'
Jeanne Greenberg Rohatyn, New York City. Interview by Leah Singer. Photography by Jason Frank Rothenberg. 2016.

'I know architects who don't ever build their own homes because they would only notice the flaws. They say it takes seven times rebuilding your home before it's perfect, but I think I like the little mistakes.'
Sonya Park, Tokyo. Interview by Misha Janette. Photography by Marco Velardi. 2009.

'My goal was to make the house look like you could not imagine it any other way.'
Jeremiah Goodman, New York City. Interview by Pilar Viladas. Photography by Jason Frank Rothenberg. 2014.

'I think because I was publicly known as this character that was so different from me, I have always made my home very personal in order to remind me of who I am and what I like and what inspires me.'
Justin Bond, New York City. Interview by Michael Bullock. Photography by Nacho Alegre. 2010.

Lawrence Weiner, New York City. Interview by Leah Singer. Photography by Mark Borthwick. 2017.

Opposite: 'I tailor-made this world for me.'
Ricardo Bofill, Barcelona. Interview by Arquitectura-G. Photography by Adrià Cañameras. 2013.

'You just have to keep going. Take ownership! Take ownership! Take ownership! You don't have to just lie down.
You're the boss, apple sauce. Believe in yourself without question!'
Flawless Sabrina, New York City. Interview by Michael Bullock. Photography by Vincent Dilio. 2017.

'I've also realised that as a collector you run the risk of having your things control you.'
Zoe Bedeaux, London. Interview by Anja Aronowsky Cronberg. Photography by Juergen Teller. 2011.

Opposite: 'Later, when I saw this house in Arles, it was like looking at his place … It reminded me of the decay and the atmosphere
of Cy Twombly's place. I feel very attached to that emotional combination.'
François Halard, Arles. Interview by Nacho Alegre. Photography by François Halard. 2013.

'With my books I want to spur children on to ask their parents questions. Of course it's really tough on the parents. Maybe that's one of the reasons the pedagogues don't like my work that much, because they have no answers. We simply have no answer to the absurdity of all the problems we are facing.' Tomi Ungerer, Cork. Interview by Daniel Morgenthaler. Photography by Nicole Bachmann. 2010.

Felix Friedmann, London. Interview by Marco Velardi. Photography by Felix Friedmann. 2008.

Makoto Orui, Paris. Text by Makoto Orui. Photography by Ola Rindal. 2011.

'You dress up to be pretentious and the same goes for your house: you decorate it to show that you are rich.'
Christophe Lemaire & Sarah-Linh Tran, Paris. Interview by Emanuele Fontanesi. Photography by Ola Rindal. 2012.

'I no longer place cities at the top of a hierarchy of coolness, but looking out at the bridges and seeing those weird downtown buildings all lit up at night is a distinctly urban experience.'
Ezra Koenig, New York City. Text by Ezra Koenig. Photography by Nacho Alegre. 2009.

Opposite: 'I feel almost more at home here when I step outside, rather than in through the front door … I like that this is a working area; the fields change with the seasons. I love watching the crops change. The roads get very muddy with the work and the enormous tractors that use them, and I like that, too.'
Margaret Howell, Bawdsey. Interview by Hugo Macdonald. Photography by Osma Harvilahti. 2016.

'This idea of being an American socialist, which I really am, was that you work very hard, but your children do not have to be like you in order to survive …
I'm very proud of my daughter, it's by luck we have a reasonable relationship, but she is not there because of me.'
Lawrence Weiner, New York City. Interview by Leah Singer. Photography by Mark Borthwick. 2017.

'It's a ground-floor apartment so I don't have to share an entrance with anyone, which I love. After living in several doorman buildings and always having to greet them so you don't seem like a jerk, or talk to other people in the elevator, it's a relief.'
Chloë Sevigny, New York City. Text by Chloë Sevigny. Photography by Lele Saveri. 2009.

'To be honest, I somehow have less knowledge about books today than I did five or six years ago, only because I deal with so many … There's that old romantic notion of working in a bookshop where you sit around reading all the books all day long. There's no time for that.'
Conor Donlon, London. Interview by Adam Saletti. Photography by Wolfgang Tillmans. 2012.

'I like to have instruments around, I'm always switching them out, but they're always around. I also have a separate room with stuff that should just be for adults, instrument-wise. I know it sounds strange, like all the handcuffs and whips and stuff I keep separate.'
Jason Schwartzman & Brady Cunningham, Los Angeles. Interview by Dean Kissick. Photography by Jason Nocito. 2016.

'I used to think that relaxation was a total fallacy invented by lazy people and that it was an excuse for not doing anything ...
I was obsessed with the idea of constantly feeling euphoric or dynamic.'
Matthew Stone, London. Interview by Dean Kissick. Photography by Brett Lloyd. 2015.

'I quite like the combination of that coming of age and not coming of age … When I was at school we would roam the streets at night, but my mum always made us pretty dresses. I remember being dressed for parties, but often a bit wrong. I like that idea of things that are beautiful but a little off.'
Molly Goddard, London. Interview by Danielle Pender. Photography by Angelo Pennetta. 2016.

'When you're young and gay, all the rules are rewritten. You're told something your whole life, and then you're like,
"Wait, all that shit that everybody told me, like that I'm supposed to be with a girl, is just bullshit".'
Ryan McGinley, New York City. Interview by Hillary Navin. Photography by Petra Collins. 2015.

Opposite: Rachel Korine, Nashville. Photography by Marlene Marino. 2012.

'In other families you gather to play games—Scrabble, or something like that. In our family we gather every evening to brainstorm new business ideas. That's where I get all my ideas from!'
Rafael Horzon, Berlin. Interview by Helena Nilsson Strängberg. Photography by Franziska Sinn. 2014.

'I used to draw with the evening news on. I have a drawing of Patrice Lumumba from that time. I probably loved the word and plus he was cool looking with his fez and all. I was always drawing James Bond in his car. I really wanted to be a spy. Drawing was a way of fantasising, which it still is.'
Duncan Hannah, New York City. Interview by Jim Walrod. Photography by Richard Kern. 2016.

'Since camp was John's intention from the beginning, it allowed us to design freely and flamboyantly, never bound by any rules of good taste.
Think of it this way: most drag queens don't seriously try to look like a real woman. They take liberties to create a woman who is way over the top.
The Belvedere is an oversized beach house in Palazzo drag.'
Craig Eberhardt & Julian Dorcelien, Fire Island. Interview by Michael Bullock. Photography by Wolfgang Tillmans. 2017.

'This eclectic mix is very common in Russia ... It usually happens when the guy has a limited amount of money and starts to renovate the flat.
He can change the kitchen and bathroom, but not the living room or wallpaper.'
Gosha Rubchinskiy, Moscow. Interview by Alexander Elzesser. Photography by Gosha Rubchinskiy & Pavel Milyakov. 2010.

Arielle Holmes, Los Angeles. Text and photography by Marlene Marino. 2015.

Paz de la Huerta, New York. Photography by Marlene Marino. 2014.

Opposite: 'There's hardly a children's book of mine without an element of fear, of something bad happening. I'm doing
a big campaign now in France, going around schools asking children what they're scared of.'
Tomi Ungerer, Cork. Interview by Daniel Morgenthaler. Photography by Nicole Bachmann. 2010.

'As a foreigner in Deià you could do anything you wanted. A lot of parties, boozing, and drugs. There was a "happening" down at the beach every day when I was a child, and there was always chess, poetry, people looking for Jesus Christ, people coming back from India with transparent tunics.'
Feature on Abdul Mati Klarwein, Deià. Interview with Balthazar Klarwein & Laure Klarwein, by Luis Cerveró. Painting by Abdul Mati Klarwein. 2016.

Opposite: 'One thing I found cute at the time was that he set down a structure with wooden poles and newspapers in roughly the size of the prospective building, and he went across the valley to see it from a kilometre away to decide if it wasn't too disruptive to the landscape—if it fitted well.'
Feature on Philolaos, Saint-Rémy-lès-Chevreuse. Interview with Marina Tloupas, by Yorgo Tloupas. Photography by Frederike Helwig. 2015

'Back at the apartment where Arielle is temporarily staying with her boyfriend, an attractive black hypnotist, and his roommate, a flaxen dominatrix, the photoshoot unfolds seamlessly.'
Arielle Holmes, Los Angeles. Text and photography by Marlene Marino. 2015.

'Even when I was living in Greece, sometimes I'd go spend a couple of nights in a hotel. Just for a change of scenery. It's the thing of having room service
or being able to go downstairs to the lobby for a coffee and be in a totally different environment.'
Yorgos Lanthimos, London. Interview by Evangelia Koutsovoulou. Photography by Juergen Teller. 2012.

Opposite: Maria Vittoria & Giorgio Backhaus, Filicudi. Text by Giorgio Backhaus. Photography by Maria Vittoria Backhaus. 2010.

'To visit the church [that we moved into] we had to go to the Sunday service. The Catholic community had moved out but they were renting it out to a free church, so we had to go on Sundays to visit and secretly take some pictures.'
Johann & Lena König, Berlin. Interview by Helena Nilsson Strängberg. Photography by Nan Goldin. 2016.

'I hang upside down on it.'
Kembra Pfahler, New York City. Interview by Michael Bullock. Photography by Vincent Dilio. 2016.

'This building was basically rundown with a lot of artistic characters in it, mostly gay guys, and they ventured into this neighbourhood,
collected themselves into this building.'
Christiaan Houtenbos, New York City. Interview by Wes Del Val. Photography by Daniel Riera. 2014.

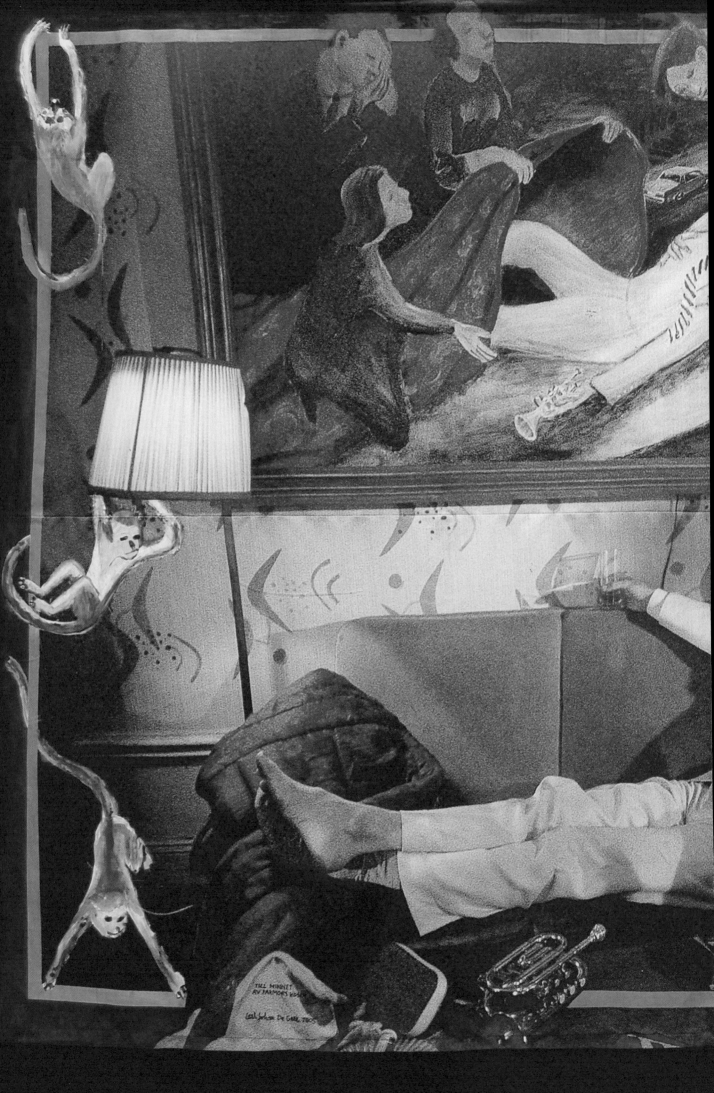

Carl Johan de Geer, Stockholm. Interview by Helena Nilsson Strängberg. Artwork by Carl Johan de Geer. 2010.

Tiphaine De Lussy, Selles-sur-Cher. Text by Emily King. Photography by Louise Melchior. 2010.

Opposite: 'To rent: fully renovated church, high ceilings, king-size bed, high-speed internet, projector, gym, and washer/dryer in crypt.
House rules: no religious events. This is (not yet) an official rental, so please be discreet with neighbours. If asked, say you're staying with friends.'
Rate your host: 10 unique rental opportunities. Text and painting by Jean-Philippe Delhomme. 2017.

'Could I live in this room? Probably not.'
Jeremiah Goodman, New York City. Watercolour by Jeremiah Goodman, Diana Vreeland garden in hell sitting room. 2014.